The Lion is the Lamb:

A Study of the King of Kings, His Glorious Kingdom, and His Promised Return

By Andrew Roberts

Published by
Spiritbuilding Publishing
15591 N. State Rd. 9
Summitville, IN 46070

Spiritual "equipment" for the contest of life.

Printed in the United States of America

Roberts, Andrew
   The Lion is the Lamb: A Study of the King of Kings, His
      Glorious Kingdom, and His Promised Return

www.Spiritbuilding.com

Author's Note

This effort is for the glory of Jesus Christ, savior and king.

I thank my elders and brethren at the Jackson Heights church of Christ for their encouragement, support, and being kingdom-minded.

I thank my brother, Jonathan, for his collaboration and suggestions. I thank the Spiritbuilding team for their encouraging words as well as confidence in the material.

I thank my wife, Julie. Her wisdom, patience, strength, and talents are rich blessings to me and our daughters, Erin and Olivia.

I hope this Bible study will be an aid to those who are confused by the shifting programs and plans of so-called prophecy experts concerning the "End-Times." Dates as well as date-setters come and go but Scripture is true, Jesus is king, and the messianic kingdom of Old Testament prophecy is the New Testament church of Christ. Just approach the following pages with an open mind and an open Bible and you'll see that Calvary's lamb is the kingdom's lion. The Lion is the Lamb!

Andrew Roberts
October 2008

Contents

Introduction

Lesson 1

The Bible is Our Kingdom Guide

The Kingdom of Christ

The Second Coming

The End Times

Few themes capture the imagination of believers and unbelievers alike. Yet the exploration of grand subjects such as the reign of Jesus or the world's end fuels interest, excitement, and anticipation. Surely the sensational speculation of today's "prophecy experts" causes some of the current End Times appetite. But who needs them? The pure Word of God on these matters is wonderful and simply amazing.

The Lion is the Lamb invites all to open their Bible and contemplate the King of kings—the creator and redeemer, the savior and judge. Jesus Christ is glorious! And all who believe that Jesus is the Christ desire a place in His kingdom. This study touches on issues that stretch from eternity to eternity, and the Bible is our guide for it all.

The fact is, while "Christendom" is mostly united in the conviction that Jesus is the Christ, there is great controversy among adherents about His kingdom. Is the kingdom spiritual, encompassing aspects of heaven and earth? Or is the kingdom strictly physical, pertaining solely to earth? Has the kingdom been established? Are Christians citizens of it today? Or, as others say, is the kingdom yet to be established? If the kingdom is yet to be established, shall it only come gradually by the proclamation of the gospel over the world? Or must Christ's kingdom come about suddenly after the world is shocked by "the Tribulation" and a bloody Armageddon?

This is just a taste of the confusion and contradiction that exists concerning the kingdom. But what is so frustrating is that all these views (and many more) on Christ's kingdom come from people who profess to read, believe, and obey the Bible. Does the Bible reveal all of these different plans and programs for Christ's kingdom? The simple answer is "no."

It has been said that, "You can make the Bible say anything you want it to." Now, if we handle it accurately and honestly, the Bible will only "say" what God intends for it to "say." However, the Bible warns that it can be misused and abused (2 Peter 3:15-16; Revelation 22:18-19). Only when Scripture is twisted, misrepresented, or altered (by addition or subtraction) can people make the Bible fit their notions. But the Bible, itself, is consistent and true.

Current disagreements and contradictory teachings about Christ's kingdom are a sign of people mishandling Scripture in some way; they do not show the Bible to be untrustworthy (2 Peter 3:15-16). As dispensationalist Dwight Pentecost writes:

> No question facing the student of Eschatology is more important than the question of the method to be employed in the interpretation of the prophetic scriptures. The adoption of different methods of interpretation has produced the variant eschatological positions and accounts for the divergent views within a system that confront the student of prophecy.[1]

So Bible believers draw various conclusions about Christ's kingdom and the End Times because they do not read the Bible alike. They employ different methods of interpretation. Therefore, as we begin, it is important to consider how we shall approach the Scriptures in our study of *The King of Kings, His Glorious Kingdom, and His Promised Return.*

Respecting the Bible

This Bible study rests on the conviction that the Bible is:
- **Inspired (2 Timothy 3:16; 2 Peter 1:20-21)**
- **Sufficient (2 Timothy 3:16-17; 2 Peter 1:3l; Jude 3)**
- **Inerrant (John 8:32; 14:6; 16:13; 17:17)**

The Bible is Inspired. The word inspired means "God breathed." The Bible is revelation from God. The Scripture is what He has chosen to tell us. While God used many men to be writers, there is only one author of the Bible. Therefore, what the Bible says about the king and the kingdom is what God said on the matter.

The Bible is Sufficient. It is all that God has purposed to tell us to complete us for doctrine, worship, life, godliness, and equipment for every good work. While it may not answer every question we can conceive, it certainly provides all that is necessary for the good of our souls. And there is no other revelation or source of religious authority that we should turn to apart from the Bible. Therefore we must content ourselves with what the Scriptures say about the king and the kingdom—that is the entire truth of the matter.

The Bible is Inerrant. The Bible is true, without error. This is all or nothing. Either it is the very word of God, as it claims, or it is a horrific pack of lies. We don't pick and choose which verses are "really" from God and which parts have been added by men. It is God's Word. Therefore we can trust what the Scripture says about the king and the kingdom.

From this high regard for Scripture we move forward with the desire to speak "as the oracles of God" (1 Peter 4:11) on the subject of Jesus Christ and His kingdom.

Understanding the Bible

God has not given us His word to confuse us or deceive us (1 Corinthians 14:33; Titus 1:2). The point of revelation is to make things known. We do not need a special method of Bible study or interpretation designed especially for our subject. Some may wonder if it is necessary, given the wild teachings about the kingdom in respect to Jesus' Second Coming or the End Times. But like all other Bible studies, what is required is simple diligent work at reading the Scripture and handling it accurately (2 Timothy 2:15).

Luke 10:25-37 gives Jesus' model for discerning the meaning of God's word. When He was questioned by a lawyer (a professional religious scholar) about understanding the Scriptures, Jesus provided the process of discernment that anyone can master.

First, Jesus asked, "What is written in the law?" (Luke 10:26). What does the Scripture say? This teaches Bible students about observation. Reading the Bible for all its worth begins with close observation of the text. We must read and reread passages to notice all that is there.

Second, Jesus asked, "What is your reading of it?" (Luke 10:26). What does the Scripture mean? This shows Bible students about interpretation. Based on all that has been observed, we determine the meaning.

Third, Jesus directed, "do this" (Luke 10:28), and, "Go and do likewise" (Luke 10:37). This instructs Bible students regarding application. Once Christians observe what the Word says, and understand what the Word means, they are to live according to the Word!

The Importance of Observation

The Bible is literature. It should be read and interpreted as any other literary document, recognizing that there are different genres of literature. The Bible contains books of law, history, poetry, prophecy—even letters. Observing the kind of literature we are reading is fundamental to properly understanding it.

For instance, let's look at the book of Revelation. Good observation is the key to properly discerning John's message. What kind of literature is the book of Revelation? It is a book of prophecy (Revelation 1:3; 22:18-19). But notice that it is also an epistle—a letter (Revelation 1:4-6). This prophecy was written by the apostle John and addressed to seven churches in Asia (Revelation 1:1-4). This letter (like all the books of the Bible) was written for us, but it was not written to us. There is an immediate application for the seven churches of Asia. They were in the midst of trials, persecution, and tribulation (Revelation 1:9; 2:10, 13).

Notice that its message is communicated in a unique way—it is signified (Revelation 1:1). So we are told that in this letter God employed signs, symbols, and figures to communicate His Truth. Therefore, taking a wooden literalism to the book of Revelation is nonsensical. As Dr. Stafford North wrote:

> The "rule of thumb" we use in every day language is that any statement that, on its face, is absurd or extreme if taken literally, is likely intended to be a figure of speech. The sports announcer, for example, may say a basketball player is "quick as lightning" or that a tight end is "like a bullet" down the sidelines. We immediately know how to switch from the literal to the figurative. So we come to Revelation with its long list of characters and events that appear absurd or extreme if taken literally, and we take them figuratively.[2]

Furthermore, we observe throughout the letter that the things communicated would be happening soon. These things would occur within the generation of the seven churches that received the letter (Revelation 1:1, 3; 3:11; 22:6-7, 10, 12, 20). North commented on our appreciation of the timeliness of the letter so that our interpretation is not mistaken:

> In the verses where Jesus says "I come quickly," He clearly is not speaking of His second coming. If He were, He would have been mistaken, for His second coming did not happen soon after the book was written. Rather, He was speaking of His coming to carry out the promises and predictions He makes in this book… So, when Christ promises to "come quickly" in Revelation, He does not mean that His second coming will be soon. Rather, He means He will "come quickly" to carry out the promises and threats He makes in Revelation.[3]

Taken together, these observations show that interpreting the book of Revelation with wooden literalism—understanding it to forecast world events of two thousand years (or more) in the future—would be mistaken. The book of Revelation has important things to say about Christ's kingdom, but it has nothing to do with the premillennial and dispensational models of current End Times prophecy experts.

Observation will be our main tool in looking at many of the prophecies and texts for this study. We want to observe the details of a text and pay attention to its context within a chapter, within a book, and within the whole of the Bible. No portion of Scripture can be understood to outright contradict another portion of Scripture.

Tools for Interpretation

When it comes to interpreting Scripture, we need to remember that, as with all speech, everything is not necessarily literal. Speakers and writers employ symbolism, hyperbole, metaphors, and allegory. A person can easily be misunderstood when they are using a metaphor if it is taken literally. It happened to Jesus.

Consider John 2:19-20. Jesus' words were immediately interpreted by those angered with His cleansing the temple to pertain to Herod's Temple. In fact, Jesus was speaking of the temple of His body and foretelling the resurrection. Jesus was speaking truthfully but not literally. John interprets His words, and we see that Jesus was using figurative language (John 2:21-22).

Again, when Jesus referred to "that fox" Herod (Luke 13:31-32), He was not saying that the king was literally a *Vulpes vulpes* of the Canidae family. It was a figure of speech.

The Scripture itself is the best interpreter of Scripture. We can compare the usage of words or imagery in one text to its other usages throughout the Bible. We will see that much of the symbolic language in the New Testament actually appeared in the Old Testament first. By considering its use in the Old Testament, we can more easily interpret the New!

Finally, some Old Testament prophecies are identified as fulfilled in the New Testament. There are instances where the apostles or other inspired writers cite Old Testament prophecy and declare it to be fulfilled. They say, "This is That." And that settles that!

For instance, in Acts 2:16-17, Peter quotes the Old Testament prophet Joel. He says that the events of Pentecost are the fulfillment of Joel's words pertaining to "the last days." Later Peter preached to a multitude that all the Old Testament prophets, from Moses to Samuel on down, were proclaiming "these days" (Acts 3:22-24). Because the inspired apostles interpreted Old Testament "last days" language to refer to the first century events surrounding the Messiah, any prophecy expert today that goes to the Old Testament to bolster their theories about End Times scenarios are at least 2,000 years off the mark!

We must be vigilant in our observation and interpretation of the Scriptures as it pertains to Christ's kingdom. Too many have strayed away from what the Bible simply reveals on the matter. That is why there are vast differences in understanding the kingdom. That is why there is much false teaching about it.

The Compass

Many popular prophecy experts strictly associate Christ's kingdom with the End Times. They speak of the Bible as if it is a Doomsday Clock whose "signs of the times" are counting us down to the end of the world. But the Bible is no such Clock.

Instead, the Bible is a Life Compass. It shows us the way of righteousness and truth. It gives us direction for life so that we can know the true God, serve Him, worship Him, and go to be with Him in heaven. It reveals all God would have us to know about our savior, *the King of Kings, His Glorious Kingdom, and His Promised Return*. The Bible is our Kingdom Guide.

Lesson 1 Questions

1. Would you agree that people like to imagine and speculate about the kingdom of Christ? If so, why do you think this is?

2. What kinds of things have you heard self-professed Christians say about the kingdom?

3. Why is it important to study the king, His kingdom, and His promised return?

4. "You can make the Bible say anything you want it to." What must be done to the Bible in order for this statement to be true?

5. What cause did Dwight Pentecost suggest for the problem of self-professed Bible students all having different understandings of the kingdom and the End Times?

6. What does "inspired" mean as it is used in 2 Timothy 3:16?

7. What three convictions about the Bible are indispensable to respecting it as the Word of God?

8. What threefold process for discerning Scripture do we observe in Luke 10:25-37?

9. Which step (of the three) is most crucial? Why?

10. What observations are important to make when studying the book of Revelation?

11. What helps for interpretation does the Bible provide?

12. Why should we view the Bible as a Life Compass instead of a Doomsday Clock?

Lesson 2

What Is the Bible All About?

It is exciting to read about the spread of the gospel in the book of Acts. We are given fantastic insight into the message that moves men's hearts as we observe the preaching of Philip in Acts 8.

"Then Philip went down to the city of Samaria and preached Christ to them" (Acts 8:5). We may wonder what all preaching "Christ" included. However, the record explains. "But when they believed Philip as he preached the things concerning the kingdom of God and the name of Jesus Christ, both men and women were baptized" (Acts 8:12). It is evident that when Philip preached Christ, he preached:

- The kingdom of God
- The name of Jesus Christ
- Baptism

This shows us that a proper understanding and proclamation of the kingdom is as fundamental to the gospel as Christ's authority or baptism in conversion. Consequently if people are mistaken about the kingdom, then they are not truly preaching Christ. And that is serious.

Sadly, many self-professed believers in Christ would rather leave the study of the kingdom in an arena of "doubtful disputations" or "agree-to-disagree" incidentals. There are some who reason that different understandings of God's kingdom can be considered a peripheral issue, because it all has to do with things that will happen long after our lifetime. So why fuss about it?

The Bible truth of Jesus Christ and His kingdom transcends the confusing (and often revised) charts of the End Times scenarios put forth by premillennialists, dispensationalists, and the like. The subject of the kingdom is not only important to preaching the gospel, but it completely impacts how people read the Bible. The way a person understands the kingdom changes the way they understand the Bible. Dispensationalist John Walvoord rightly pointed this out:

> There is a growing consciousness within the church that premillennialism is more than a dispute on the twentieth chapter of Revelation and that instead it involves a system of interpretation of the entire Scripture from Genesis to Revelation.[4]

For example, premillennialists, and dispensationalists teach that the Bible is all about promises that God made to Abraham and Israel that He has still yet to fulfill. Once a National State of Israel occupies all the promised land of Canaan, and Jesus Christ Himself is sitting on a literal throne in Jerusalem, and a great golden Temple is standing, and daily sacrifices are performed, and all around is peace for exactly 1,000 years, then God will be found true and all His promises, prophecies, and purposes will be fulfilled. To teach such a scheme clearly involves a unique "system of interpretation of the entire Scripture."

Some warn against this system.

> The doctrines of the future 1000 year reign are dangerous because they view the church as an 'episode' unseen in its full beauty by the prophets. The conviction of many is that the purpose of the church is to help the Jew obtain the kingdom; not to offer Christ's salvation to the Jew through the fold of the church.[5]

So the fair question is raised: What is the Bible all about? Reading from the book of Genesis to the book of Revelation (using "Observation, Interpretation, and Application" from lesson 1), we find that the Bible reveals God's plan for the salvation of sinners in Jesus Christ.

God created a world that was good. And His first children, Adam and Eve, were good (Genesis 1:31). Yet they were tempted, and choosing to transgress God's single rule, they sinned (Genesis 3:1-13). But Adam and Eve did not depart the Garden of Eden before God declared that sin and evil would one day be crushed (Genesis 3:15). Throughout the ages that followed, events were prophesied, occurred, and recorded in Scripture that brought about the promised Seed that would crush the devil and deliver lost sinners. While these things were occurring, it was never fully understood just how God would do it. But by the gospel of Jesus Christ, the whole plan was made clear (1 Peter 1:10-12).

God Fulfilled the Promises to Abraham

Abraham was an important figure in the accomplishment of God's plan of salvation for sinners. By studying God's dealings with Abraham, we learn many valuable lessons. For instance, we learn that God is faithful and true. We see a great example of what it means to live by faith. And we gain the foundation by which God would accomplish His grand scheme of salvation: His three promises to Abraham.

God called Abraham out of his homeland, Ur of the Chaldeans, to go to a land that he had never seen (Genesis 12:1-9; Acts 7:1-4; Hebrews 11:8). God made three promises to Abraham:

1. **The Nation Promise.** "I will make you a great nation" (Genesis 12:2). (See also Genesis 15:5.) God said He would make Abraham into a great nation. His descendants would be multiplied like the stars in the sky or the sands of the seashore. This was quite a promise, because Sarah, his wife, was barren and Abraham was already seventy-five years old (Genesis 11:30; 12:4).

2. **The Land Promise.** "To your descendants I will give this land" (Genesis 12:7). (See also Genesis 15:13-21; Acts 7:5-8.) While Abraham did not own Canaan, He was told that his numerous posterity—the large nation descending from him—would posses all of the land of Canaan. In fact, God marked off the territory of the Promised Land. Abraham's descendants would receive the land "from the river of Egypt to the great river, the River Euphrates" (Genesis 15:18).

3. **The Seed Promise.** "And in you all the families of the earth shall be blessed" (Genesis 12:3). (See also Genesis 18:18; 22:18; Acts 3:25-26; Galatians 3:7-9, 16.) One descendant would arise from Abraham's posterity who would be a blessing and savior to all the nations of the earth—the entire world!

The Scriptures record how God faithfully (though in His time) kept every promise to Abraham. From Abraham's sole son of promise, Isaac, came Jacob (later Israel), and from Israel came the twelve sons, eventually the twelve tribes. By the days of Moses, it was recognized that God had multiplied the descendants of Abraham into the nation of Israel (Deuteronomy 1:10; 10:22). The first promise was fulfilled. In fact, the post-exile Levites of Nehemiah's day said this promise was fulfilled (Nehemiah 9:23).

The land promise was also fulfilled. Stephen's sermon in the book of Acts teaches us that the land promise was time sensitive. There was a particular time and circumstance that the descendants of Abraham would endure prerequisite of God giving them the land (Acts 7:5-8):

- Abraham's descendants would dwell in a foreign land.
- The foreign power would bring them into bondage.
- The foreign power would oppress them for 400 years.
- God would judge the nation that oppressed Abraham's nation.
- After that they would come out and serve God in "this place" (i.e., the Promised Land).

Stephen said, "But when the time of the promise drew near which God had sworn to Abraham, the people grew and multiplied in Egypt till another king arose who did not know Joseph" (Acts 7:17-18). Clearly God gave the time when the second promise would be fulfilled—upon the Exodus from Egypt! (See also Deuteronomy 1:6-8.)

Not surprisingly, that is when the Scripture says that God's second promise to Abraham was fulfilled—when the Israelites, under Joshua's leadership, took the land of Canaan by God's direction. "So the LORD gave to Israel all the land of which He had sworn to give to their fathers, and they took possession of it and dwelt in it" (Joshua 21:43). (See also Joshua 21:44-45; 23:14; 24:13; Acts 7:45.)

The Israelites did not keep their territory in peace, though. Throughout the book of Judges and 1 and 2 Samuel, they are constantly warring with the nations that they failed to utterly expel in their initial conquest. While God's promise to give the land was unconditional and fulfilled, their keeping the land was dependant on their faithful service to God (Joshua 23:14-16; Deuteronomy 28:15-68). If they transgressed His Law, practiced idolatry, or acted like the nations around them, then God would expel them from the land. They would "perish quickly from off the good land" He had given them (Joshua 23:16, NASB). How could they perish off of something they did not possess?

Historically, Israel was removed from the Promised Land (2 Kings 25:21). Nebuchadnezzar held all the land—the very boundaries marked out by God to Abraham—when He took Judah into captivity (2 Kings 24:7). In fact, Daniel appropriated Moses' language of blessing and cursing and confessed that the Lord had "confirmed" it through the Babylonian captivity and exile (Daniel 9:10-17). Before that occurred, however, it was declared that God had faithfully given the descendants of Abraham all that had been promised. Solomon's territory was recorded in the Bible. "So Solomon reigned over all kingdoms from the River to the land of the Philistines, as far as the border of Egypt. They brought tribute and served Solomon all the days of his life" (1 Kings 4:21). (See also 1 Kings 4:24-25; 2 Chronicles 9:26.) Just like the first promise to Abraham, the post-Babylonian-exile Levites of Nehemiah's day said the land promise was fulfilled (Nehemiah 9:7-8, 23).

So who are modern "prophecy experts" to come along and say that God has never truly fulfilled the Land Promise to Abraham? For instance, Charles M. Neal wrote:

> It is a scriptural and historic fact that Abraham and his
> seed have never occupied the promised land in the fullness of

its limits. In fact, they never entered but a portion of it when they came out of Egypt... This larger land of promise will be re-allotted to restored and converted Israel, according to the promise and covenant made unto the fathers... That this re-allotment is a past fact no one will affirm. It awaits the restoration of Israel and the coming age.[6]

A basic tenet of modern dispensational doctrines is that God has yet to fulfill His second promise to Abraham. Yet as we have read, the Holy Spirit throughout both Testaments said that He has. Assertions like Neal's make God out to be untrustworthy and a liar! But observing the Scripture shows that God is faithful and keeps His promises.

The dispensational preoccupation with Palestine is a major departure (and regression) from New Testament Christianity. In John 4:19-24, Jesus showed that the worship of God would no longer be tied to a particular location or geography, such as the Jerusalem temple. Worship would be in spirit and truth. But dispensationalists contend that Christianity and all the world is heading back to that corporeal significance—the earthly temple is more important than the spiritual temple. Someday Israel will get all their land, they say. The reign of God and the worship of God will be tied to the land—Jerusalem. This thinking is backwards (Galatians 3:24-25).

Finally, in the New Testament, we learn of God fulfilling the Seed Promise. The Seed that would bless all nations is Jesus Christ (Acts 3:25; Galatians 3:16). Jesus was the prophesied One. By His gospel, people from every nation can have the forgiveness of their sins, reconciliation to the one true God, and an eternal home in heaven (Romans 1:16; Mark 16:15-16; 1 Peter 1:3-5).

It Is All About Jesus

The first two promises that God made to Abraham and fulfilled prepared the way for the third. There needed to be a place and a people where the Messiah would originate. Many scriptures make it clear that God's eternal purpose—what the Bible is all about—is Jesus Christ making the way of redemption for lost humanity (Acts 2:22-24; 1 Peter 1:18-21; Revelation 13:8; Ephesians 3:8-12). The Bible is all about Jesus Christ:

- The Old Testament is coming up to Christ.
- *Matthew – John* is the coming of Christ.
- Acts is coming into Christ.
- *Romans – Jude* is continuing in Christ.
- *Revelation* is saints crowned with Christ.[7]

Jesus Never Sought an Earthly Kingdom

The modern millennial contention is that the Jewish Messiah (Jesus Christ) must reign over an earthly kingdom in Palestine. Since the Bible is all about Jesus, we should be interested in what He said He would do when He came to Earth. What did Jesus say His mission was? Did Jesus tell people that He came to established an earthly kingdom?

Jesus came preaching the gospel of the kingdom (Matthew 4:23; Mark 1:14; Luke 8:1), and He even said that it was near or "at hand." Does that mean He intended to establish an earthly kingdom? He told Pilate He was the King of a kingdom, but that His kingdom was not of this world (John 18:36-37). Instead of Pilate feeling threatened by a rebel King, he sought to release Jesus, John 18:38. That does not sound like an earthly king.

If Jesus had desired the earthly kingdom of Israel, it was offered to him—twice! The devil offered Him all the kingdoms of the world if Jesus would only worship him (Matthew 4:8-10). That included earthly Israel. But He resisted the devil. On another occasion excited crowds sought to take Jesus and forcibly crown Him as king of Israel. "Therefore when Jesus perceived that they were about to come and take Him by force to make Him king, He departed again to the mountain by Himself alone" (John 6:15). We might understand why Jesus would not want the devil giving Him a kingdom, but why desert the people if your mission is to be their earthly king?

Jesus did say He came to:

- Fulfill all the Law and the Prophets (Matthew 5:17)
- Bring a sword of division (Matthew 10:34-39)
- Build His church (Matthew 16:18-19)
- Shed His blood for a new covenant and the remission of sins (Matthew 26:28)
- Preach (Mark 1:38)
- To serve and give His life a ransom for many (Mark 10:45)
- To be killed and rise on the third day (Luke 18:31-33)
- Seek and save the lost (Luke 19:10)
- Bring abundant life (John 10:10)
- To be glorified (John 12:23)
- Be the light of the world (John 12:46)
- To be king of a kingdom not of this world and bear witness of the truth (John 18:36-37)

What is not accomplished? He accomplished everything intended. In no way was His mission or God's eternal purposes in Him thwarted!

It is shocking that a believer could entertain the notion that Jesus failed in any aspect of His Messianic work. Lest we come to the shameful conclusion that Jesus' first advent was a cosmic bungle, making Messianic prophecies into false prophecies, we ought to reexamine just what exactly it was Jesus came to do and just what exactly is written of Christ's kingdom in all that the Scriptures say.

Kingdom is just one term used by the Holy Spirit in the Bible to speak of that body of people who are the redeemed. This assembly of people has remission of sins in Christ. The Christ and His people go together. Jesus is king and His people are those translated into His kingdom (Colossians 1:13-14). Jesus is the head, and His people are the body, the church (Ephesians 1:22-23; 5:22-23). Jesus is the bridegroom, and the church is the bride (Revelation 21:9; 22:17). Jesus is the Shepherd, and they are the flock (John 10:11-16). Jesus is the cornerstone of the foundation, and His people are the building (Ephesians 2:19-22).

All of these designations have their place in describing the arrangement purposed in eternity, prophesied and prepared for throughout the Old Testament, and accomplished by Jesus Christ and the gospel. The Bible unfolds God's plan of redemption and brings the offer of pardon and new life in Christ's kingdom to us today.

What we believe about the kingdom is essential to the gospel of Jesus Christ and influences the way we understand God, the work of Jesus Christ, and the entire Bible. God did not fail to deliver on His promises when He said He would deliver. Jesus did not fail or even postpone His Messianic work, but fulfilled every prophecy—on time—as written. Jesus is the one and only Messiah, and His church is the one and only Messianic kingdom.

Lesson 2 Questions

1. What three themes did Philip proclaim when preaching "Christ"?

2. Why is a proper understanding of Bible teaching about "the kingdom" necessary for Christians today?

3. How does a premillennial view of the kingdom (or any other millennial view) impact the way people read the Bible?

4. In your own words, what is the Bible all about?

5. What three promises did God make to Abraham?

6. What significance are the three promises to a study of "the kingdom"?

7. What Bible evidence shows that the nation promise was fulfilled?

8. What Bible evidence shows that the land promise was fulfilled?

9. Why could the land promise not be fulfilled in the modern era, say 1948, or even yesterday?

10. What Bible evidence shows that the Seed promise was fulfilled?

11. Do you think Jesus intended to establish an earthly kingdom of Israel at His first advent? Why or why not?

12. Name some things that Jesus said He came to do. Did He accomplish them?

13. If Jesus did not accomplish all that He intended, or left some Messianic prophecies unfulfilled, how would that reflect upon Him?

14. Explain how these designations all speak of the same assembly of redeemed people and their relationship to Jesus.
    - King and Kingdom

    - Head and Body

    - Christ and Church

Part I

The King of Kings

Is Jesus of Nazareth the Messiah?

Is Jesus of Nazareth the Messiah? Put another way, is Jesus of Nazareth the Christ? Perhaps Christians do not use the word "Messiah" with the same frequency as the word "Christ," but it is the same question. The inspired apostle John wrote that "Messiah" (Hebrew for "anointed one") is accurately translated "Christ" (Greek for "anointed") in John 1:41 and John 4:25. These words describe the same appointed Deliverer. And the question is: is the Jesus we read of in the gospels this promised and prophesied Savior—the Messiah (Matthew 1:21; Luke 2:11)?

This may seem a strange question for Christians to consider. After all, Christians call themselves…well…Christians—followers of the Christ (Acts 11:26). And no sinner becomes a Christian without confessing that they believe Jesus is the Christ (Acts 8:36-38; Romans 10:9-10; 1 Timothy 6:12-13).

But Christianity hinges on Jesus' identity. He has to be the Messiah or it is false and futile. Surprisingly, many professed Christians' view of the kingdom does great harm to the king. Among premillennialists and dispensationalists, Jesus is said to be Christ, but it is qualified. Most of them say that He is the Messiah of prophecy, but He has yet to fulfill all the Old Testament Messianic prophecies—especially those that pertain to the kingdom. As they see things, Jesus had two missions on earth. The primary mission was to establish an earthly kingdom of Israel that would rule the world. Supposedly, Jesus desired to fulfill all the Messianic prophecies at His first appearance but could not because Israel rejected Jesus as their Messiah and stymied that mission. So God put all of the kingdom prophecies on hold. Then Jesus commenced a second mission: He went to the cross, rose again, and established His church. They contend that the church was unknown to Old Testament prophecy but fills the gap of time until Jesus returns again and finally establishes His kingdom in Israel.

Lesson 3 - Is Jesus of Nazareth the Messiah?

What kind of Messiah only fulfills half of the Messianic prophecies? What kind of Messiah does not finish His Messianic work? Did the first century Jews really have the power to thwart God's intentions and force Him into activating a "Plan B"?

Was Jesus the Messiah because of the Jews or because of God? Was Jesus the Messiah because the Jews said He was? Did He answer to the Jews so that, when the Jews rejected Him, He ceased being Messiah and forfeited a kingdom? Or was Jesus the Messiah because God said He was? Jesus established His kingdom regardless of men receiving Him or rejecting Him. The Bible shows us this. When Jesus sent out the seventy to preach, He told them that the kingdom of God was near those people— whether the people liked it or not (Luke 10:8-12). Mankind's disposition toward the kingdom of God does not prevent the kingdom of God.

Instead of accepting systems that rob Christ of His glory as Messiah, we should determine to understand the prophecies of the Bible in a manner consistent with His Messiahship. When Jesus tells us that His kingdom is not of this world (John 18:36), we should accept what He said and seek to learn more of a spiritual kingdom. Instead, most premillennial and dispensational teachers add, "But SOMEDAY His kingdom WILL BE of this world." This is sad and misleading, because the Scriptures never say anything of the kind.

Dispensationalist and Zionist John Hagee presents an alarming teaching in his book, *In Defense of Israel*, to harmonize the dispensational doctrine of Jesus' earthly kingdom in Israel and the lack of its establishment in the New Testament. Hagee denies that Jesus was the Messiah. Instead he suggests that Jesus came the first time to be the Savior of the Gentiles and establish His church. When Jesus comes again, He will be the Messiah and establish His throne in Jerusalem to reign for 1,000 years.

Hagee wrote, "[T]here is not one verse of Scripture in the New Testament that says Jesus came to be the Messiah... Jesus refused by his words or actions to claim to be the Messiah of the Jews..."[8] On the contrary, there is much New Testament Scripture testifying that Jesus is the Messiah.

Andrew told Simon Peter that he had found the Messiah—Jesus (John 1:41-42). Jesus revealed He was the Messiah to the Samaritan woman (John 4:25-26). It is important to note that in both instances John equates "Messiah" and "Christ." When it is preached or confessed that "Jesus is Christ," it is preached or confessed that "Jesus is Messiah." It is the same thing. If Jesus is not Messiah, then He is not Christ.

Several people in the Scriptures confessed their conviction that He was the Christ—the Messiah. Peter (Matthew 16:16), Nathanael (John 1:49), Martha (John 11:27), and John the Baptist (John 1:34) all confessed Him as Messiah. If Hagee is right, Jesus should have corrected them and told them that He was there to save Gentiles, not rule Israel. If Hagee is right, Jesus was a tad duplicitous on His identity with His disciples. But maybe such disciples were jumping to conclusions. Where would they get the idea that Jesus was the Christ?

Did Jesus, Himself, claim to be the Messiah? Absolutely! Read Luke 4:16-21. Jesus publicly read the Messianic prophecy of Isaiah 61:1-2 and said that it is fulfilled! Notice the content of what He read:

- The Spirit of the Lord is upon Jesus.
- Jesus is anointed (recall what "Messiah" means!).
- Jesus will preach the gospel to the poor.
- Jesus will heal the broken-hearted.
- Jesus will proclaim liberty to the captives.
- Jesus will cause the blind to see.
- Jesus will liberate the oppressed.
- Jesus will proclaim the acceptable year of the Lord.

Does that sound like a claim to be the Messiah?

When John the Baptist was imprisoned, he sought reassurance that Jesus was the Messiah (Luke 7:18-20). Jesus performed various miracles in the presence of John's messengers and told them to report all that Jesus did as evidence that He was the Messiah (Luke 7:21-23).

So what about Jesus' signs? Hagee contends that Jesus did not perform miracles to prove to the Jews He was their Messiah. "If God intended for Jesus to be the Messiah of Israel, why didn't he authorize Jesus to use supernatural signs to prove he was God's Messiah, just as Moses had done?"[9] Hagee does not deny that Jesus performed miracles; he says that Jesus kept His miracles secret and warned people not to tell others about them. Therefore He did not do open signs that would heighten His public profile and show He was the Messiah.[10]

The events of John 9 could not be much higher profile though. Jesus healed a man who was blind from birth to teach the people that He was the light of the world. The formerly blind man went and testified before his family and the Pharisees that Jesus must be from God. The chapter concludes by the seeing man being cast out of the synagogue but confessing he believed that Jesus was the Son of God.

When Jesus healed in the synagogues on the Sabbath, it was always public and controversial. But He showed that He had the power and the authority for He was Lord of the Sabbath.

Secret miracles surely puts Peter in an awkward place when He preached on Pentecost to a crowd of out-of-towners that God had attested to Jesus by miracles, signs, and wonders (Acts 2:22). If Hagee is correct, then these people would be clueless about Jesus' miracle ministry. But in fact, Peter did not even give examples of the many miracles; he simply said, "as you yourselves also know." The bulk of Peter's sermon was on the resurrection, that great and final sign of the Messiah.

When Jesus was feeding five thousand people, it could hardly be said He did it in secret. And multitudes followed Him because His gracious miracles supplied physical needs (John 6:26). But when Jesus tried to lead them to a spiritual understanding of His work and kingdom, many of the crowds departed from Him (John 6:66).

But Jesus actually appealed to His miracles as proof that He was the Christ (John 5:36). And the gospel writers, like John, recorded many of His signs to demonstrate to all – Jews and Gentiles – that Jesus is the Christ, the Messiah (John 20:30-31; John 1:41; 4:25).

Hagee's theory shows the same resistance toward a suffering Messiah that the first-century Jews held. Hagee wrote, "It was God's sovereign will for Jesus to die from the very dawning of time. Had Jesus permitted himself to become the reigning Messiah to the Jews, he would have missed the sovereign will of God for his life."[11] Hagee also wrote, "Jesus had to live to be the Messiah…it was God's will for Jesus to die from the beginning… it was Jesus' intention to be obedient unto death…"[12]

Can Jesus NOT be the Messiah because He was crucified? Or is Jesus the Messiah BECAUSE He was crucified and then rose on the third day! Is it inconceivable that the Messiah be killed? Must the Messiah exclusively experience victory? All of the apostles preached that Jesus had to suffer so He could be victorious! In fact, we would not know for certain that Jesus is the Messiah apart from His resurrection (Romans 1:4). And there could be no resurrection apart from the cross! Peter's conclusion to the Pentecost sermon is that Jesus is Lord and Christ (Acts 2:36). He told those Jews assembled that their Messiah was Jesus. Peter told them that the Messiah had come, that God had planned for Him to suffer in the manner He had. They had lawlessly crucified their Messiah and God had raised Him from the grave (Acts 2:22-24). All this was done according to prophecies in the Scriptures. So Peter quotes from Joel 2, Psalm 16, and Psalm 110.

Later, in Acts 26:22-23, we see that the apostle Paul stood on the same ground as Peter. Paul testified before King Agrippa that he preached the fulfillment of the Old Testament Scriptures. Notice that included that the Christ (Messiah) would suffer, would rise from the dead, and would proclaim light to both Jews and Gentiles. It is amazing that a professed Christian could say Jesus was not Messiah because He died. This completely ignores the Old Testament passages that dictated His suffering and His resurrection!

Hagee goes so far as to exclude Israel from the gospel. He wrote, "The message of the gospel was from Israel, not to Israel!"[13] And he presses the idea that Jesus never intended to be Messiah to the Jews and that He has another plan in store for saving the Jews—the gospel simply was not for them. This notion is not at all consistent with the New Testament.

Lesson 3 - Is Jesus of Nazareth the Messiah?

Jesus came preaching the gospel to Jews (Mark 1:14-15, 35-39). Jesus limited His earthly ministry to nearly exclusive dealings with "the lost sheep of Israel" (Matthew 15:22-24). Peter preached on Pentecost to Jews that Jesus is Lord and Christ—the only Messiah is the Jewish Messiah (Acts 2:36-38). Peter made it clear that the Messiah came to Israel first, because God had promised Him through Abraham and foretold Him through the prophets (Acts 3:25-26). The message of salvation, which is the gospel, has been sent to the children of Abraham as well as Gentiles (Acts 13:46; Romans 1:16). Jesus was a servant to the Jews, on behalf of God's truth (Romans 15:8).

There is only one gospel (Galatians 1:6-8). The gospel was foretold in the Old Testament Scriptures (Romans 1:1-5). The gospel is the power of God unto salvation for everyone who believes, for the Jew first and also for the Greek (Romans 1:16). It is indefensible to say that the gospel was not to Israel. It was to Israel FIRST and then the rest of the world (Acts 1:8).

The final stunning statements to be dealt with here regarding Hagee's Messiah doctrine declare that the Jews never rejected Jesus. Hagee wrote, "The Jews were not rejecting Jesus as Messiah; it was Jesus who was refusing to be the Messiah to the Jews…They wanted him to be their Messiah, but he flatly refused...He refused to be their Messiah, choosing instead to be the Savior of the world."[14]

The above statements prompt us to consider the relationship of Jesus to the Jews. Clearly not all of the Jews rejected Jesus. The apostles, the first disciples, as well as the great church in Jerusalem were all Jews. But at the same time, the Jewish leadership and the majority of the people did reject Jesus as the Messiah. In fact, the Sanhedrin sentenced His death for claiming He was the Messiah (Mark 14:61-64). Jesus lamented over Jerusalem for her rebellion and resistance of God's messengers—and that included Him (Matthew 23:37). And it was a Jewish mob that yelled to Pilate, "His blood be on us and on our children" (Matthew 26:25). Peter indicted the people for this rejection and hostility toward the Messiah and showed that Jesus would forgive them (Acts 2:23, 36-41). All of these things demonstrate Jews rejecting their Messiah. And 2,000 years later, one of the contentions of Judaism is that Jesus of Nazareth is not the Christ.

Jesus only refused to be an earthly king of Israel (John 6:15). Hagee makes earthly rule the work of the Messiah. The Bible makes spiritual rule the work of the Messiah. His kingdom is not of this world (John 18:36). Jews and Gentiles alike have the same opportunity by the gospel to be citizens of His kingdom. Jesus has not refused to be the Messiah to any man. He is the Messiah for every man. Because there is only one Messiah, one Christ, to save Jew and Gentile alike, and He is Jesus of Nazareth.

Hagee's anti-Christian notion that Jesus came once to be a suffering Savior for the world and will come again to be a victorious Messiah over Israel is only a slight repackaging of Judaism's view of Jesus. As *Fausset's Bible Dictionary* explained in its "Messiah" entry:

> The rabbis got over the Messianic prophecies which prove Jesus to be Messiah by imagining a Messiah ben Joseph who should suffer, distinct from Messiah ben David who should reign; but the prophecies of the suffering and glory are so blended as to exclude the idea of any but one and the same Messiah (compare Isaiah 52:7,13-15; 53).[15]

How alarming that a self-professed Christian would turn a blind eye to the New Testament, so as to lie and say Jesus is not the Christ (Messiah). This is destructive heresy, and he stands with the modern religion of Judaism to deny the Lord (2 Peter 2:2).

"Who is a liar but he who denies that Jesus is the Christ? He is antichrist who denies the Father and the Son" (1 John 2:22).

But we should follow the example of the apostles, never ceasing to declare that Jesus is the Christ (Acts 5:42). The apostles stood on solid ground when they made their declarations, because Jesus showed them that He was the Messiah the Scriptures revealed (Luke 24:27, 44; John 5:46). The apostles preached the fulfillment of the Old Testament in Jesus Christ (Acts 3:18; 17:2-3; 18:27-28). Their listeners could examine the Scriptures and see if Jesus of Nazareth fulfilled them or not (Acts 17:11). He did fulfill it all—both the suffering and the victory of the Messiah.

Lesson 3 - Is Jesus of Nazareth the Messiah?

Messianic prophecy is powerful evidence that demonstrates Jesus is the Christ. The Jews did not question the inspiration or accuracy of the Scriptures, and a Messiah was clearly prophesied. One person would fulfill all of the prophecies. The prophecies constituted a picture of the Messiah: where He would come from and what He would do. Here are a few examples:

- His lineage (Isaiah 11:1)
- His mother (Isaiah 7:14)
- His birthplace (Micah 5:2)
- His preaching (Isaiah 61:1-2)
- His miracles (Isaiah 61:1-2)
- His suffering and death (Isaiah 53)
- His resurrection (Psalm 16:10)

Not only do the prophecies show us what the Christ would do, but they also present a window of time that the Christ must appear. Some Messianic prophecies were time sensitive. This means that if they were not fulfilled in the time they said they would be, they will never be fulfilled and they are in fact false prophecies. God does not postpone fulfilling prophecies. Either a prophecy is fulfilled and thus truly from God or it is not (Deuteronomy 18:22).

For example, the Messiah will appear only after His forerunner appears (Isaiah 40:3-5; Malachi 3:1; 4:5-6). Jesus Christ, as well as the inspired New Testament writers, identified the forerunner of the Messiah as John the Baptist (Matthew 3:1-3; 11:7-15). Now, if the Messiah has not come, we must vigilantly look for a forerunner first. However, the Bible says that all the prophecies of the forerunner were fulfilled in the person and ministry of John the Baptist. If the Messiah did not come after the forerunner, but the forerunner has come and gone, then it is too late for the Messiah to come. There will be no Messiah.

Another example of time sensitive prophecy is that the Messiah must come while the temple of Jerusalem is standing (Malachi 3:1; Haggai 2:6-9; Daniel 9:26). This means that the Messiah had to come by 70 A.D. because that's when the Romans destroyed Jerusalem and the Temple, which has never been built again. If the Messiah did not come before the Temple was destroyed, then it is too late for the Messiah to come. There will be no Messiah.

A final example in this area is the Messiah's lineage. The Messiah had to be a descendent of Abraham (Genesis 22:18), Judah (Genesis 49:9-10), Jesse (Isaiah 11:1), and David (2 Samuel 7:12-13). The Bible contains Jesus' genealogy to demonstrate fulfillment of these promises and prophecies (Matthew 1:1-17). Jesus declared that He was the Messiah of prophesied lineage (Revelation 3:7; 22:16). But all Jewish written genealogies were lost when Rome destroyed Jerusalem in 70 A.D. This means that if the Messiah was not Jesus and did not come before A.D. 70, it is impossible to demonstrate fulfillment and meet this criteria.

Jesus is the Christ. Those who deny it and are yet looking for the Messiah to come are looking in vain. But God has given many proofs to trust that Jesus of Nazareth is the Messiah.

Lesson 3 Questions

1. Why does Christianity hinge on the identity of Jesus?

2. What does "Messiah" mean?

3. What New Testament word means "Messiah"?

4. Did Jesus claim to be the Messiah?

5. Did Jesus do the signs of the Messiah? Give some examples.

6. What New Testament event fulfills prophecies that the Messiah would live *and* die?

7. Was the gospel for Israel? Explain.

8. Give examples of Messianic prophecies that Jesus fulfilled?

9. If Jesus was not the Messiah, is it possible that the Messiah will come in our lifetime or the future? Why or why not?

10. Is it a serious thing to confess or deny that Jesus is Messiah? Why or why not?

The Lion is the Lamb

John looked for a lion but found a lamb. It happened in the book of Revelation. Notice Revelation 5:1-7—especially verses 5 and 6.

> But one of the elders said to me, 'Do not weep. Behold, the Lion of the tribe of Judah, the Root of David, has prevailed to open the scroll and to loose its seven seals.' And I looked, and behold, in the midst of the throne and of the four living creatures, and in the midst of the elders, stood a Lamb as though it had been slain, having seven horns and seven eyes, which are the seven Spirits of God sent out into all the earth (Revelation 5:5-6).

John gazed toward the throne, as instructed, intending to see the lion that the patriarch Jacob prophesied long ago (Genesis 49:9-10). Jacob's words were one of the oldest Messianic prophecies in Scripture. They dealt with the Messiah's kingship and rule. They identified the Jewish tribe that the Messiah would descend from: Judah. The symbolic image of a lion (Revelation 5:5) corresponds with the "Shiloh" (meaning peacemaker[16]), to whom belongs the obedience of the nations (Genesis 49:10, NIV).

Yet in a throne room full of magnificent creatures (Revelation 4:6-11), John does not see the lion that he was told about; instead, a lamb is there. A lamb stood in the place of the lion—a lamb that had been killed! Hailey's comments help clarify the picture:

> "Behold" is an imperative which focuses attention on what is seen or heard: "The Lion that is of the tribe of Judah." ... This long-expected descendant of Judah, who would possess the strength of the lion, bear the scepter of rule over the peoples, and speak peace or bring rest to men, had now come: "For it is evident that our Lord hath sprung out

of Judah" (Hebrews 7:14). ...John looks to see a Lion, the symbol of majesty and power; but instead, he sees a Lamb which, though it had been slain, was now standing and living. This introduces the sacrificial and redemptive aspect of the One whom John saw. He had overcome to open the book not by the power of kingly might, but by sacrifice through love. By this He had defeated His foes and had overcome the world (John 16:33), and by this His subjects must now conquer. ... The one who rules as "the Lion of the tribe of Judah" gained that right through sacrifice, and those who rule with Him now must gain their right to rule with Him in the same manner.[17]

John looked for a lion but found a lamb. Does this mean that there is no lion? No. The lion is the lamb. The lamb's sacrifice and victory over death is the source of the lion's peacemaking power and authority to rule. "Lion" and "lamb" are paradoxical images and John sees the power of the lamb.

First, notice that the lamb had seven horns (Revelation 5:6). In biblical numerology, seven is the number of the divine or perfection. Seven horns communicate complete power or omnipotence. Second, the lamb had seven eyes. They communicate complete knowledge or omniscience. This lamb has purchased a people by His blood that is made up of every tongue, tribe, people, and nation. He has made them a kingdom of priests (Revelation 5:9-10, NASB). He is worthy to rule and has a kingdom to rule. The lion is the lamb, King Jesus. But He did not appear as John had expected to see Him.

Behold, the King

This episode in the book of Revelation is typical of how many people have viewed the King of kings and His glorious kingdom. The first century Jews that Jesus walked among looked for a lion! But instead, they saw a lamb. Nevertheless Jesus was the "Lion of the tribe of Judah," and many called Him, "King."

For instance, the angel Gabriel told Mary that Jesus would "reign over the house of Jacob forever and of His kingdom there will be no end"

(Luke 1:33). Also wise men from the East had traveled great distances in search of the "King of the Jews" to worship Him (Matthew 2:2). One of the disciples, Nathanael, called Jesus "the King of Israel" (John 1:49). Even the Sanhedrin accused Jesus before the Romans of calling Himself "a king" (Luke 23:2). And Pilate sought to release the One he called "King of the Jews" (John 18:39). Finally, the words on the cross labeled Jesus, "Jesus of Nazareth, the King of the Jews" (John 19:19).

But did this king ever look like a king? When the wise men traveled a great distance to worship the Christ child, they did not find Him at Herod's palace, but in the small village of Bethlehem. There was nothing outwardly regal about His birth or childhood. Growing up in Nazareth did not put Him on the fast track to world leadership. Nathanael was originally skeptical of Jesus simply because He hailed from that village (John 1:45-46). The Sanhedrin fiercely opposed Jesus' kingship. He certainly did not look much like a king as He was "tried" and abused in their midst. Pilate did not view Jesus' claim to kingship as a threat to Rome. King Jesus' subjects would not rise up to physically defend their king (John 18:36-37). Could a person look less kingly than enduring the shame and torture of crucifixion?

He is the lion. He is the king. He is called the king. But He never looked like an earthly king! He was not born into golden palaces or to a life of ease. He was born in a stable and laid in a trough. He grew up as a carpenter's son, learning a trade. The insignificant Nazareth was the background of His childhood—not Rome, Alexandria, Athens, or Jerusalem. There's no record of Him owning any property. In fact, He had nowhere to lay His head (Luke 9:57-58). He was poor.

When He came on the scene, preaching the kingdom was at hand, He never stirred up the people to revolt against the government. And there were plenty of Jews who were ready for the revolution to begin and Rome to be ousted. He did not raise an army. He did not lead guerilla raids against Roman posts. He did not even teach civil disobedience. Instead He told His followers to pay their taxes, honor the laws of the land, and pray for their enemies (Mark 12:13-17; Matthew 5:41, 43-48). What kind of king is this?

While the kings of the earth demand to be served by their subjects, King Jesus served His people, His disciples, and the whole world.

> But Jesus called them to Himself and said, 'You know that the rulers of the Gentiles lord it over them, and those who are great exercise authority over them. Yet it shall not be so among you; but whoever desires to become great among you, let him be your servant. And whoever desires to be first among you, let him be your slave -- just as the Son of Man did not come to be served, but to serve, and to give His life a ransom for many' (Matthew 20:25-28).

Not only was Jesus the king that did not look like any earthly king, but He could not be an earthly king of the Jews. He came from the wrong family.

Bible students are aware that Jesus could not be an earthly priest of the Jews because He came from the wrong tribe. When God instituted His Law at Mt. Sinai, He chose the tribe of Levi to be the priests and ministers of His worship and tabernacle (later, the Temple). But Jesus was from the tribe of Judah. "For it is evident that our Lord arose from Judah, of which tribe Moses spoke nothing concerning priesthood" (Hebrews 7:14).

Yet Jesus is the Christian's high priest. How can that be? There was a change of law. Under the new covenant of the gospel, Jesus is a priest according to the order of Melchizedek and not the order of Aaron (the Levite, and Israel's first high priest) (Hebrews 7:11-19). Melchizedek was a priest of the Most High in the days of Abraham (Genesis 14:18-20). But not only was Melchizedek a priest, he was a king (Hebrews 7:1-3). He was both priest and king. But the Law of Moses did not establish such a dual office for earthly Israel. Priests came from Levi, and kings came from Judah.

Just as Jesus was from the wrong *tribe* to be an earthly priest in Israel, He descended from the wrong *family* to be an earthly king over Israel. Jesus was from the right tribe to be a king (Judah), but He was from the wrong family to ever rule over Israel.

Jesus was a descendant of one of the last kings of Judah, Coniah, also called Jeconiah and Jehoiachin (Matthew 1:12). Coniah was wicked in God's eyes (2 Kings 24:9). God moved the prophet Jeremiah to say that Coniah should be written down childless and that no man of his seed shall prosper, sitting upon the throne of David and ruling in Judah (Jeremiah 22:24-30). Concerning Coniah, Wallace wrote:

> Jeremiah, the prophet, said no man of his seed should prosper sitting on David's throne and ruling any more in Judah. What does that have to do with the question of Christ sitting on David's throne? Just this—Jesus Christ was of the fleshly seed of Coniah. When the Lord said, "Write this man childless," it does not mean that Coniah was congenitally childless—the names of his sons are given in the Old Testament record, as well as the New Testament genealogies. Coniah had sons; he was not childless physically; but the Lord said, "write this man down childless." That meant that he should not have a successor on David's throne; that Coniah would be the last man to occupy the fleshly throne of David.[18]

From Kings to Carpenters

Have you ever wondered why it is that Jesus' earthly father, Joseph, was a poor carpenter and not a prince? After all, he was a descendant of King David. But he also descended from Coniah.

David's earthly throne became extinct when Nebuchadnezzar deposed Coniah in 597 B.C., taking him into exile and placing Zedekiah on the throne (2 Kings 24:10-20; Jeremiah 24:1). Zedekiah was a puppet-king of Nebuchadnezzar's choosing and never truly sovereign (Jeremiah 37:1-2). His eleven-year tenure ended in 586 with Nebuchadnezzar's third and final invasion of Judah (2 Kings 25:1-10).

One of Coniah's grandsons, Zerubbabel, was appointed a governor by Cyrus the Great to lead the first band of post-exilic Jews to Judah and rebuild the Temple. But Zerubbabel was not sovereign. He answered to Cyrus. Furthermore, Zerubbabel's children did not succeed him in his office of governor. Different emperors established different leaders. For instance, Nehemiah, a cupbearer, was put in charge of restoration efforts in Jerusalem during the reign of Artaxerxes I. Zerubbabel's descendants faded into obscurity. World empires swept over Judah: Persia, Greece, Ptolemies, Seleucids, and eventually Rome. Along the way, the office of high priest with his moral authority eclipsed the kingship of Judah. The Jews were never an independent nation again.

These world events fulfilled the prophet's message. Jeremiah's words meant that Coniah's seed could not rule and prosper over Judah. That means Jesus could not be an earthly king! Wallace summarized:

> Now since Christ is the seed of Coniah, and no man of his seed can sit on David's throne and rule any more in Judah, it follows that Jesus Christ cannot occupy the throne of David on earth. But the prophets said that Jesus Christ the son of David, should occupy David's throne. Since it cannot be done on the earth, it follows that Jesus Christ would occupy David's throne not on earth, but in heaven. And that is exactly what Peter affirms in Acts 2:30.[19]

Where does that leave Jesus? How can He be king without breaking the scripture? Again, the covenant changed, and Jesus is after the order of Melchizedek, a priest and king. Jesus is a spiritual king over a spiritual kingdom (Hebrews 7:1-3). God's word is true. The lion that some looked for came as a lamb, not what they expected. Nevertheless, the lion is the lamb!

The Hebrew writer shows that Melchizedek was an Old Testament type and that Jesus Christ is the fulfillment, the antitype. But if people were looking for Jesus to be an earthly high priest, He could not be according to the Word of God. Likewise, if people were looking for Jesus to be an earthly king over Israel, He could not be according to the Word of God. But the Messiah is both priest and king, as the Scriptures foretold (Zechariah 6:12-13), just not in the fleshly manner that people assumed.

From where Jesus sits now, on the throne of David, at the right hand of God, He is Lord of lords and King of kings—far greater than any earthly king could ever be (Acts 2:29-31; Mark 16:19; Hebrews 1:3). In the glory and grandeur of heaven, He is still the king that doesn't look like a king, for He is too great and grand and glorious to be considered on par with any earthly king.

Lesson 4 Questions

1. What does a lion symbolize? Why would Jacob call Judah a lion's whelp (Genesis 49:9)?

2. What does a lamb symbolize? Why did John the Baptist call Jesus a lamb (John 1:29)?

3. How can Jesus be both the lion and the lamb?

4. Are there biblical instances when people expected one thing from Jesus but got something else?

5. Who called Jesus a king?

6.   Did He ever look much like an earthly king? Explain.

7.   Why couldn't Jesus be an earthly priest in Israel?

8.   Why couldn't Jesus be an earthly king in Israel?

9.   How is it that a descendant of David (like Joseph) would be a carpenter and not a prince?

10. How is it, then, that Jesus is priest and king today?

Risen Christ, Reigning King

Jesus Christ is the Messiah (John 4:25-26; Acts 2:36). He is both priest and king, after the order of Melchizedek (Hebrews 5:5-11; 7:1-3). He is not priest according to the Law of Moses because those priests had to be of the tribe of Levi, and Jesus' earthly ancestry was the tribe of Judah (Hebrews 7:13-14). Yet He had to be priest to fulfill Old Testament Scriptures (Psalm 110:4; Hebrews 7:21). So what occurred that allowed this to transpire? A change of the law. "For the priesthood being changed of necessity there is also a change of the law" (Hebrews 7:12). By the new covenant or New Testament, Jesus Christ is the high priest in heaven, though He could never be a high priest to God on earth, under the Old Testament (Hebrews 4:14-15; 7:20-9:28).

Likewise, Jesus could not be king over Israel according to the prophet Jeremiah because Jesus was an earthly descendant of Coniah (a.k.a. Jeconiah; a.k.a. Jehoiachin), the wicked king whose earthly dynasty was divinely removed (Jeremiah 22:30; Matthew 1:11). Coniah had children, but none of Coniah's seed would sit on the "throne of David" and rule. That marked the end of the earthly throne of David. Yet the Messiah has to occupy the "throne of David" (2 Samuel 7:11-17; Psalm 89:3-4, 27-29, 35-36). How can Jesus do this without breaking the scripture (John 10:35)? It is impossible for Jesus to reign on a fleshly throne of David as a priest and king without breaking scripture. Jesus Christ occupies David's throne in heaven, not on earth (Acts 2:30). He reigns from heaven, not on earth (John 18:36).

Jesus is as much king today in heaven as He is priest today in heaven. He is both at once, being after the order of Melchizedek, King of Salem and Priest of the Most High God (Hebrews 7:1-3). In fact, this is the only understanding that allows Zechariah's Messianic prophecy to be fulfilled in Jesus.

Then speak to him saying, 'Thus says the Lord of hosts, saying: "Behold, the Man whose name is the BRANCH! From His place He shall branch out, And He shall build the temple of the Lord; Yes, He shall build the temple of the LORD. He shall bear the glory, And shall sit and rule on His throne; So He shall be a priest on His throne, And the counsel of peace shall be between them both"' (Zechariah 6:12-13).

A priest would never sit on a throne, ruling God's people in Israel. Priests came from one tribe and kings from another. But in heaven, Jesus is priest and king. He is the priest ruling on His throne, the throne of David— in heaven! Jesus is the lion, the reigning king!

As we have already noted in this study (and will address in greater detail), there are many professed Christians today that question, if not deny, that the kingdom of Christ has come. Some preach that Jesus intended to do something in the first century that he just could not do: establish a physical kingdom over Israel. For example, consider comments from John MacArthur's sermon, "Kingdom Parables":

> If Jesus came to offer the Kingdom, if Jesus came to bring His Kingment to earth, to reign and to rule, and to establish that which was promised and they refused Him and refused His Kingdom, what then happened to the Kingdom?... Because, you see, the Kingdom cannot come, listen carefully to this, until the nation Israel receives the King. And so, at this point, the Kingdom had to be postponed in terms of its full fulfillment... Because they rejected the King, the Kingdom in its full fulfillment had to be postponed. And it had to be postponed to a future time. What time? The second coming of Christ. You see, that's why Christ is coming a second time, to bring the Kingdom that was refused the first time... And that's why He's coming back and will again offer that Kingdom and this time it will be received.[20]

MacArthur defines the "full fulfillment" of the kingdom as "that Kingdom which comes to pass on the earth both internally, that is in the hearts of believing people, and externally as Christ rules and reigns as King on earth."[21] MacArthur leaves no doubt that he believes Jesus' intention was (and yet remains) to reign over the world from an earthly kingdom in Israel. However, the first century Jews thwarted Jesus' mission. "Now, that is what He would have done when He came the first time had they believed. Had they believed, they would have received the King internally and they would have received the Kingdom externally. But they did not believe. And so, the fullest fulfillment was postponed."[22]

These quotations are simply examples of what millennialists (pre-, post-, or dispensational) have been preaching for 200+ years. But immediate problems arise with this teaching.

First, it makes Jesus less than what the Bible says He is. Jesus said He has "all authority in heaven and on earth" (Matthew 28:18 see also Ephesians 1:20-23; Colossians 1:16-18). There is no superlative for "all." If He now has "all" authority in heaven and on earth, how can it be said that He lacks any aspect of authority (like rule of an earthly kingdom) if He intended to possess it? MacArthur's theory means that the Messiah would have multiple reigns, first spiritual and then corporeal. But the Scriptures only speak of one reign. As Boles wrote:

> Christ has all authority now (Matt. 28:18); angels and authorities are now "subject to him" (1 Pet. 3:22); he does not wait until he comes again to receive this authority; he is reigning now in his kingdom (1 Cor. 15:25; Heb. 2:8); his present reign will continue in his kingdom until the last enemy is destroyed; then he will deliver the kingdom to God. He will not reign *after his present reign ceases, for there is only one reign of Christ mentioned in the Scriptures.* His principles, spirit, and love will continue in force until the last enemy is conquered. It is a travesty on Christ and his kingdom to suppose that his kingdom is to be like that of Alexander the Great, or Xerxes, or any other mighty murderer on earth... the Bible mentions only one reign for Christ and that he is now reigning, and hence no other reign is to be given him.[23]

Second, how can one explain that all along Jesus intended to have an earthly kingdom in Israel when He never sought it, but rather avoided it (John 6:15)? He specifically said His kingdom was not of this world (John 18:36). Where in the New Testament did Jesus say He came to establish an earthly kingdom? If He had come to establish an earthly kingdom and reign upon an earthly throne of David, He would have transgressed the Scriptures pertaining to Coniah, His ancestor (Jeremiah 22:30; Matthew 1:11-12). But Jesus never transgressed the Word of God—He was sinless (1 John 3:4; Hebrews 4:15).

Finally, what will God do differently in the future than He did in the past to ensure Israel's faith and establish the kingdom (as millennialists say is necessary)? Will He send prophets? Will there be miraculous signs? Would He even send His Son? Jesus' parable of the wicked vinedressers makes it clear that God has done all He will ever do for Israel in sending the Messiah (Luke 20:9-19).

According to Luke 10:5-12, the coming of the kingdom never rested on the people's acceptance or rejection. Whether the villages received the message or not, the kingdom of God had come near to them. Furthermore, their judgment would be harsher than Sodom's for rejecting the kingdom. The kingdom is not postponed by unbelief; rather, unbelievers are judged for their rejection! In fact, those living in first century Palestine witnessed the kingdom present with power (Mark 9:1). Far from being postponed 2,000+ years, the kingdom was established with Jesus' first advent. If not, Jesus either knowingly or unknowingly lied. What Christian can accept this?

The kingdom question creates a kingship question. If (as some claim) Jesus failed to establish the kingdom He desired in the first century, what is He the king of? If He has no kingdom, or at least not the "full" kingdom, then how can He be a king or a "full" king—like that kind of king that would be called "King of kings"? MacArthur's theory says Jesus is a king by virtue of His identity, but makes Him currently a refugee, a king in hiding, "the King in absentia."[24] Jesus is not now the full king—He someday will be, a king in fact and in act. Is this so? Let us consider the reign of King Jesus.

The Promise of an Eternal Throne

King David of Israel desired to build God a house, a temple for the ark. While his intentions were noble, God did not want a "man of war" to construct the holy site in Jerusalem. But God promised David (through the prophet Nathan) that He would make David a "house"; that is, He would give David a tremendous lineage. We read of this encounter in 2 Samuel 7:11-17. Ultimately, God promised David that the Messiah would descend from him and reign on his throne (2 Samuel 7:11-17; Psalm 89:3-4, 27-29, 35-36). Observe the six promises of 2 Samuel 7, along with their New Testament fulfillment in Jesus Christ.

1. When David rests with his fathers… (2 Samuel 7:12). David would be dead and resting when God brought this thing about. Peter makes this very point when preaching Christ on Pentecost—David is dead and buried in a known tomb (Acts 2:29).

2. God will set up David's seed (2 Samuel 7:12). Jesus is the seed of David, according to the flesh (Romans 1:3; Matthew 1:6). Matthew's genealogy is quite telling on the "seed." He draws attention to Abraham, as well as David, for both were made the "seed" promise (Matthew 1:1, 17). And Jesus is that seed (Galatians 3:16). Peter said David understood that the "fruit of his body" was the Christ (Acts 2:30).

3. God will establish His kingdom (2 Samuel 7:12). The kingdom of the seed of David will be established. Gabriel announced to Mary that her yet unborn son, Jesus, "will be" given the throne of His father David and "will reign" (Luke 1:32-33). And Peter preached that it had been done by God for Jesus (Acts 2:30, 32-35). If Jesus is seated on David's throne, then He is reigning and His kingdom is established. In fact, after Acts 2 and the announcement of Christ upon David's throne, the kingdom is not spoken of as "coming." Instead we see that first century Christians were called into the kingdom (1 Thessalonians 2:12), had been transferred into the kingdom of the Son (Colossians 1:12-13), and were partakers of the kingdom (Revelation 1:6, 9). The church of Christ is the Messianic kingdom of prophecy.

4. The Seed will build a house for God (2 Samuel 7:13). The church is the house of God (1 Timothy 3:15; 1 Corinthians 3:16-17; Ephesians 2:20-22; Hebrews 3:6; 1 Peter 2:5).

5. God will establish the throne of His kingdom forever (2 Samuel 7:13). Peter declared that Jesus was seated on David's throne in heaven (Acts 2:29-36). Some today reject that Christ is on David's throne. They say that Jesus is on His own throne and won't be on David's throne until He establishes an earthly kingdom and rules from Jerusalem. However, the throne of David was never about a literal chair. Recall that Solomon sat on David's throne (1 Kings 2:12). But at the same time Solomon was seated on Jehovah's throne (1 Chronicles 29:23). The "throne" is simply a figure for rule—kingly authority. Throne means the right to rule God's people. God ruled Israel (God's throne), David had the rule of Israel by God's hand (David's throne), Solomon had the rule of Israel, so he is said to be seated in Jehovah's throne and David's throne at once. In the New Testament we learn that Jesus is seated on His own throne (Revelation 3:21), Jehovah's throne (Revelation 3:21), and David's throne (Luke 1:32; Acts 2:30-31) at the same time. It is rule! God promised such rule to the seed of David, and Jesus is the fulfillment. As Simpson explained:

> The Bible traces the kingdom from its promise to fulfillment in view of one throne to be occupied. Whether it be called the throne of Christ or the throne of God, it is the same throne upon which David and Solomon reigned as occupants. The same throne which had its preparatory stages among fleshly Jews is now occupied by Christ in its spiritual fulfillment. God assigned the throne to David, and David sat upon it as an occupant. Solomon also sat upon the throne of David; but at the same time, we are told he sat upon God's throne. So David and Solomon both sat on God's throne as occupants...1 Kings 2:12... 1 Chronicles 29:23... God's throne, David's throne, Solomon's throne, and Christ's throne are all the same throne.[25]

The kingdom of God and the kingdom of Christ are inseparable (Ephesians 5:5). The church of God and the church of Christ are inseparable (1 Thessalonians 1:1). Likewise the throne of God and the throne of Christ are inseparable (Hebrews 1:8; Revelation 3:21).

6. God will be the seed's father and the seed will be God's son (2 Samuel 7:14). This is ultimately fulfilled in Jesus Christ, the Son of the living God (Hebrews 1:5; Matthew 3:17; 17:5).

The Messiah took the throne of David, the eternal throne, upon His resurrection and ascension to heaven (Acts 2:29-36). He is not a refugee king, "in absentia," pining for the day when the Jews will receive their Messiah and He can finally commence His full reign. He is risen, and He reigns! Peter's Pentecost sermon—along with a host of other New Testament scriptures—demonstrates that David's expectation for his "seed" was realized. Jesus reigns now!

Evidence of a Reigning Messiah

Christ's kingdom is not of this world (John 18:36). Therefore, it should not be expected that His kingdom boundaries be marked off with physical signs like the kingdoms of this world. In other words, there are no fences, border patrols, checkpoints, port authorities, or customs agencies that we can point to as evidence for the Messiah's kingdom or His active reign.

But He rules in the hearts of men—those men who gladly yield to His leadership (Luke 17:20-21). His kingdom territory is expanded one soul at a time as sinners convert to Christianity and become disciples. The collection of those individuals—the saved—is His kingdom, His church (1 Thessalonians 2:12; Colossians 1:13; Revelation 1:6. 9). His kingdom does not bear colors for identification; they bear fruit of the Spirit. His kingdom does not master carnal weapons but spiritual warfare.

The real evidence of Jesus' actual and current reign is the exercise of His authority. In other words, is Jesus acting as king? Beyond any doubt, a king has taken control of the government when things are done in his name and by his authority. From the Day of Pentecost forward, terms of pardon for the sins of all men have been preached in the name of the Lord

Jesus Christ (Acts 2:36-41; 4:10-12; 5:30-31; 10:43; 13:44-47; 19:4-5; 28:25-31). If Jesus is not king, in fact, then the apostles should not have preached that repentance or baptism or anything else be done by His name because of His authority. But He is king now. Thus, "Whatever you do in word or deed, do all in the name of the Lord Jesus" (Colossians 3:17).

Christ's Return and His Reign

While it is rejected that Christ is coming again to finally establish an earthly kingdom, it is in no way denied that Jesus shall return. But what impact does the second coming have on Christ's kingdom?

First, it needs to be established that there is no New Testament scripture that says Jesus will set one foot on the earth again. Even 1 Thessalonians 4:16-17, which mentions the Lord descending from heaven, does not say that He touches the earth. Rather, it says that the saints rise to meet Him in the air and be with Him.

So what does occur at Christ's Second Coming, pertinent to His reign? Read 1 Corinthians 15:22-28. We learn that at Christ's Second Coming, the final enemy, death, will be conquered by the resurrection of all the dead. The text says that Jesus reigns until that last enemy is subdued. Then He delivers the kingdom to God, who is all and in all. So Jesus' return marks the end of His Messianic reign, not the beginning.

The question for each of us today is not, "When is the kingdom coming?" but, "Am I in the kingdom?" Because when Jesus returns for judgment, it will be too late to be saved by the Messiah and transferred into His kingdom. The membership of the kingdom will be final, and they will be handed to the Father. Will we be in that number? Only by submitting to the reigning King Jesus today!

Lesson 5 Questions

1. What was surprising about Zechariah's prophecy concerning the Messiah?

2. How did Jesus fulfill this prophecy?

3. What are some of the scriptural difficulties that arise with the teaching that Jesus intended to have an earthly kingdom at His first appearance?

4. What are some of the scriptural difficulties that arise with the teaching that Jesus must yet establish an earthly kingdom?

5. What does the parable of the wicked vinedressers show us about God's plans to bring Israel to believe in their Messiah?

6. List the six promises God made to David through Nathan in 2 Samuel 7:11-14 and show their New Testament fulfillment.

7. What is the throne of David?

8. Could Jesus be seated on the throne but not have a kingdom? Why or why not?

9. What is evidence that Jesus now reigns?

10. Will Jesus begin to reign over a kingdom at His Second Coming? Why or why not?

11. What will occur at Jesus' Second Coming that pertains to the reign of His kingdom?

Part II

His Glorious Kingdom

Kingdom: Exercised Authority or Territory?

In the first section of this book, we focused on the King of kings, Jesus Christ. We demonstrated from the Scriptures that Jesus of Nazareth is the Messiah (or Christ). This must be proclaimed and believed; denial is a lie and antichrist (1 John 2:22).

Jesus is the fulfillment of the Law and the Prophets (Matthew 5:17-18; Luke 24:44-47). He is our spiritual high priest and king—though He could be neither on earth. His is a spiritual kingdom—not of this world (John 18:36). He reigns now. He exercises His authority and has since the Day of Pentecost when the terms for salvation were proclaimed "in His name" (or by His authority). And He reigns until the resurrection, when death is swallowed up in victory, Jesus executes judgment over the living and the dead, and He gives His kingdom over to God the Father (1 Corinthians 15:22-28; John 5:26-29; Acts 10:42).

In the second section of our study, lessons will build on the truths we gained when studying Jesus and His Messiahship. For instance, some of the prophecies for the Messianic kingdom were time sensitive, like the prophecies for the Messiah, Himself. Also we learned that when the Messiah did appear, He did not look like the world expected. Those most learned in the Scriptures (scribes and Pharisees) did not receive Him; in fact, they opposed the one for which they sought. But the lion is the lamb. Likewise, the Messianic kingdom is not an earthly empire to rival or surpass Rome. King Jesus does not use military might to conquer His enemies or enslave nations (Matthew 26:50-56; John 18:36). Rather, God's plan through Christ is to win His earthly enemies over as friends and followers. As McGuiggan observed, "The King would destroy his enemies by making friends of them, by drawing them to him in reconciliation."[26] This does not take away from Christ's position as the eternal judge (2 Corinthians 5:10); it is simply to say that the role of kingdom citizens was never to physically dominate and rule over those outside the kingdom.

Lesson 6 - Kingdom: Exercised Authority or Territory?

Must "kingdom" mean an earthly empire? For the better part of the past 200 years in America, professed Bible-believing Christians have said, "yes." They teach that when Jesus returns He will set up a global, corporeal kingdom with Jerusalem as the capital. The next five lessons will show where this notion developed, as well as where it leaves the kingdom spoken of in the Bible.

But let's spend a few moments challenging the deep-seated definition (of some) that "kingdom" in the sacred text must mean an earthly empire. If a wrong notion is left unchallenged long enough, it can be difficult to correct. As Ramsey wrote, "Always keep in mind the idea that if you tell a lie often enough, loud enough, and long enough, the myth becomes accepted as a fact. Repetition, volume, and longevity will twist and turn a myth, a lie, into a commonly accepted way of doing things."[27] That is especially the case when it comes to millennial theories of Jesus' kingdom.

Kingdom Word Study

When Bible writers used the term "kingdom," they were not primarily speaking of a realm or territory, which is exactly what most people today probably think of when they hear the word kingdom. We think of the country or island that a king rules over as his kingdom. But realm was a secondary notion of "kingdom" for Bible writers. Consider the following:

Thayer's Greek Lexicon:
> Greek, basileia (Strong's # NT: 932) --
> 1) royal power, kingship, dominion, rule
> > a) not to be confused with an actual kingdom but rather the right or authority to rule over a kingdom
> > b) used of the royal power of Jesus as the triumphant Messiah
> > c) used of the royal power and dignity conferred on Christians in the Messiah's kingdom
> 2) a kingdom, the territory subject to the rule of a king

3) used in the New Testament to refer to the reign of the Messiah[28]

Vine's Expository Dictionary:
KINGDOM

basileia NT:932 is primarily an abstract noun, denoting "sovereignty, royal power, dominion," e. g., Rev 17:18, translated "(which) reigneth," lit., "hath a kingdom" (RV marg.); then, by metonymy, a concrete noun, denoting the territory or people over whom a king rules, e. g., Matt. 4:8; Mark 3:24. It is used especially of the "kingdom" of God and of Christ.[29]

Brown, Driver & Briggs Hebrew Lexicon:
Aramaic, malkuw (Strong's # OT: 4437) --
royalty, reign, kingdom
a)   royalty, kingship, kingly authority
b)   kingdom
c)   realm (of territory)
d)   reign (of time)[30]

From these definitions we can see that the primary thought of "kingdom" is exercised sovereignty or rule. Only secondarily does "kingdom" refer to a territory or realm. Scholars say the same:

Since a king cannot rule over nothing, we quite sensibly speak of who or what he reigns over as his 'kingdom'. Scholars are agreed, however, that the term speaks of 'royal authority' or 'sovereign power'. It speaks of the power or authority exercised over a realm of people rather than the territory or people itself.[31]

The primary meaning of both of the Hebrew word 'malkuth' in the Old Testament and of the Greek word 'basileia' in the New Testament is the rank, authority and sovereignty exercised by a king…First of all, a kingdom is the authority to rule, the sovereignty of a king.[32]

Lesson 6 - Kingdom: Exercised Authority or Territory?

Significantly, Theodor Herzl (1860-1904), the modern father of Zionism, understood this concept in the same way. His visionary book, *The Jewish State* (1896), called for the reunion of Jews and the creation of a sovereign state as the answer to "the Jewish question" in Europe. He wrote:

> It is true that the Jewish State is conceived as a peculiarly modern structure on unspecified territory. But a State is formed, not by pieces of land, but rather by a number of men united under sovereign rule. The people is the subjective, land the objective foundation of a State, and the subjective basis is the more important of the two.[33]

Herzl understood that possessing Palestine was not necessary for the Jews to be a nation again. He actually did not insist on Palestine at all, but favored a portion of Uganda for his people to settle. There is more about Herzl, Zionism, and the influence of dispensationalism in future lessons. This simply illustrates that exercised sovereignty or rule constitutes a kingdom and not necessarily property.

Yet today many people automatically assume that when we read "kingdom" in our Bibles it first means a corporeal realm that Jesus will one day establish, and that must endure for 1,000 years (literal 365-day periods). They say Christ's kingdom never came, so God inserted the church into His plans (mysteriously, because the Old Testament does not prophesy the church, they say) until that time when Jesus returns and finally sets up the kingdom. Currie writes in summation of this earthly kingdom view as well as its consequences:

> It meant that the Church was not God's main plan of redemption, but a parenthetical time – dubbed the "Church age" – that would eventually give way to God's *primary* plan: a corporeal reign of the Messiah over the Jews. Jews who came to God in the Millennium would never become part of the Church. They would be part of redeemed Israel, which would remain forever distinct from Christ's Bride.
> J. Dwight Pentecost wrote extensively from this perspective in the mid-twentieth century: "There are two

new covenants presented in the New Testament: the first with Israel in reaffirmation of the covenant promised in Jeremiah 31 and the second made with the church in this age. This… would divide the references to the new covenant in the New Testament into two groups" (*Things to Come* by J. Dwight Pentecost. Grand Rapids, MI: Zondervan, 1965. page 124).

This idea, when developed, lays the foundation for the rapturist belief that *most of the teachings of Jesus do not apply to present-day Christians!* Clarence Lakin assured his readers that the Sermon on the Mount has "no application to Christians, but only those who are under the Law"; that is, those Jews who will come back to God during the Tribulation and the Millennium (Clarence Lakin in *Dispensational Truth.* page 26). Although this is gospel to rapturists, to many other Christians it sounds dangerously close to blasphemy.[34]

In the words employed by Scripture, "kingdom" must first be understood as rule, exercised authority, or sovereignty. Thus we say that Jesus is king and His kingdom came. His sovereignty is not tied to physical Jerusalem or any bit of land in Palestine. He rules now in heavenly places, with all authority, over all principality, and power, and dominion that is named (Matthew 28:18; Ephesians 1:20-23; Philippians 2:9-11).

So as we read the word "kingdom" or "kingdom of God" or "kingdom of heaven," we should try first to understand the word (or phrase) to be speaking of rule or reign.

However, the word does not exclusively mean rule or reign. Context will determine the meaning of "kingdom" in a given verse of Scripture. When rule or reign does not make sense given the context, then we understand the word to mean realm or territory. McGuiggan explains such contextual clues:

> When we read that we must 'enter' the kingdom or that people may be 'cast out' of the kingdom; when we hear that people may have the kingdom 'taken from' them or 'given to' them; when we read about people being 'in' the kingdom or being 'made' into a kingdom – when we read all this, it's

hard not to conclude that the word 'means' something like 'realm' or 'territory' when a Bible writer intends it to.[35]

Even when context shows us that the accurate meaning of "kingdom" in a given verse is the secondary usage of territory or realm, there is still a mountain of scriptural evidence discouraging the notion that "kingdom" ever refers to a future, corporeal realm centered in Israel. As we shall learn in our next lesson, the Messianic kingdom of Old Testament prophecy is the New Testament church. Jesus' kingdom came. It is a spiritual kingdom. He exercises His authority (rules) from heaven and His realm is heavenly. The Christian's hope is not an earthly inheritance—that Jesus will come back down here one day and finally have His earthly realm. Instead our hope is the incorruptible, heavenly inheritance—that when Jesus comes back, it will be to take us to Him, to take us home to heaven (1 Peter 1:3-5; 1 Thessalonians 4:13-18).

Lesson 6 Questions

1. How does King Jesus desire to "destroy" His enemies (consider Colossians 1:13-14, 19-23; Ephesians 2:11-16)?

2. What is the Greek word rendered "kingdom" in our English Bibles?

3. What is its first, or primary, meaning?

4. What is the Aramaic word rendered "kingdom" in our English Bibles?

5. What is its first, or primary, meaning?

6. What is the secondary meaning of these words?

7. What is the danger of understanding "kingdom" to mean "realm" first or exclusively—or worse, to understand it to mean a literal earthly Israeli kingdom?

8. According to J. Dwight Pentecost, how many new covenants are in the New Testament? Who are they for?

9. If the separation of Christ's church and Christ's kingdom is accurate, do all of Jesus' teachings apply to present-day Christians? Why or why not?

10. How can we tell whether "kingdom" in a given verse should be understood as "rule" or as "realm"?

11. Let's practice this. Look up the following scriptures and determine whether the "kingdom" means exercised authority or if "kingdom" means territory.

    - Joshua 13:21

    - Joshua 13:30-31

    - Esther 5:6

    - Matthew 4:8

    - Mark 3:24

    - Mark 6:23

    - Psalm 103:19

    - Daniel 4:31

    - Mark 1:15

    - Mark 11:10

    - Matthew 3:2

    - Luke 21:31

12. The Christian's hope for inheritance is in what realm (1 Peter 1:3-5)?

Lesson 7

The Messianic Kingdom of Prophecy

The past two lessons have introduced the millennialists' (pre-, post-, and dispensational) teaching that the kingdom of Old Testament prophecy and the New Testament church are distinct bodies representing distinct promises of God and multiple covenants with men. The millennialist contends that Christ's church was unforeseen in Old Testament prophecy. The so-called "church age" was a mysterious dispensation—unforeseen in the prophetic scriptures. God was moved to insert it because the Jews of Jesus' day rejected their Messiah. Since they would not receive Him, they could not receive His kingdom (understood to mean a corporeal reign and territory extending from Jerusalem).

Certainly all things are possible for God (Matthew 19:26). But is it consistent with His revelation that He would not breathe a word in the Old Testament about something as significant to the New Testament as the church? The prophet Amos likely would not think so. He wrote:

"Surely the Lord GOD does nothing, Unless He reveals His secret to His servants the prophets" (Amos 3:7).

The millennialists' speculative system manifests a very low view of the church. It is preached as a gracious Plan B for Gentiles and the minority of Jews that believed in Jesus at His first advent. (One must wonder what would have become of the Gentiles had the unknown quorum of believing Jews necessary for Jesus to establish His earthly kingdom been met at His first advent.) Eventually, as their theory goes, the church will be secretly raptured away before the real fireworks start, prior to Jesus' Second Advent. But the prophetic "parenthesis" that is the "church age" has been ongoing for 2,000 years. When will God get back around to fulfilling all of the Old Testament prophecies about a Messianic kingdom? When will the Jews and the rest of the world get to know God's *real* glory, the Messianic kingdom of prophecy?

Lesson 7 - The Messianic Kingdom of Prophecy

While popular preachers on radio, television, and print media prognosticate about "signs of the times," the "imminence of the Rapture," and the "rise of the Anti-Christ," their preaching is futile. They look for the coming of that which came! They speculate on the future instead of standing on the past.

The Messianic kingdom of Old Testament prophecy is the New Testament church of Christ. The church was God's eternal purpose, not a Plan B or "parenthesis" because of disbelieving Jews (Ephesians 3:10-11)! The church is to exist forever and ever to glorify God (Ephesians 3:21). We are not told it will cease so that God can have a millennial kingdom instead of the church. It was preordained that God chose those people "in Him" (in Jesus Christ) to save (Ephesians 1:4; 2 Timothy 1:9; 1 Peter 1:20). The people "in Him" are in "His body,"—the church (Ephesians 1:22-23; 5:23). People get "in Him" when they believe the gospel and are baptized into Him (Galatians 3:26-27). When one is baptized, they are baptized into the one Body, the church (1 Corinthians 12:13). The church never ceases, and the Church is being saved!

This is the gospel that Peter preached on the Day of Pentecost. The Jews had killed their Messiah, but that did not thwart God's program of prophecy—it fulfilled it (Acts 2:23). Their sin occasioned the Messiah's greatest sign and fulfillment of prophecy, the resurrection (Acts 2:24-35). It was now incontrovertible that Jesus was the Messiah, and He reigned upon David's throne (Acts 2:30-31, 36; Romans 1:3-4). Peter invited the multitudes to be saved (Acts 2:21, 40). He specifically told them to repent and be baptized by King Jesus' authority (Acts 2:38). There was an overwhelming response, and 3,000 people were baptized (Acts 2:41)! Not only that, but when they were baptized, 3,000 souls were added to Jesus' church (Acts 2:41). The Lord added to the church those who were being saved (Acts 2:47). According to the New Testament, a soul is saved when they are added to the church.

The Acts 2 Pentecost was no "mysterious insertion" or Plan B. It was the inauguration of Christ's kingdom, the church. *Old Testament kingdom prophecy becomes New Testament church history in Acts 2!* There are a myriad of kingdom prophecies that find their fulfillment on the Acts

2 Pentecost. However, we will content ourselves with examining a handful for the purpose of this lesson.

Here is an equation that might help us remember the fulfillment of Christ's kingdom on the Day of Pentecost:

Daniel 2 + Isaiah 2 + Joel 2 = Acts 2

Daniel 2:27-45

Daniel 2 presents a dire situation for the wise men of Babylon. King Nebuchadnezzar had been afflicted by a troubling dream, and he demanded to know what the dream meant. While any of the soothsayers of the court would have been glad to tackle the symbolism of the king's dream (Daniel 2:4), Nebuchadnezzar made it especially difficult: the interpreter must first tell him what he dreamt, then tell him what the dream meant (Daniel 2:5-6). When the magicians balked at this, the king commanded all the wise men of Babylon to be killed (Daniel 2:12-13). But God moved His prophet Daniel to make known the dream and the interpretation (Daniel 2:19, 27-45).

Nebuchadnezzar saw a great image—a large statue. Daniel described the statue from top to bottom:
- Its head was made of fine gold.
- Its chest and arms were made of silver.
- Its belly and thighs were made of bronze.
- Its legs were of iron, and its feet were a mixture of iron and clay.

Then a stone was cut out without hands and struck the image in the feet of iron and clay. The fine metals of the statue were crushed together into dust and blew away. The stone that had struck the feet of the statue remained and grew into a mountain that filled the earth (Daniel 2:35).

Daniel's inspired interpretation assures the king that this dream is prophetic; it deals with events that will transpire after the king and his empire are gone. Notice:

- "He has made known to King Nebuchadnezzar what will be in the latter days" (Daniel 2:28).
- "About what will come to pass after this" (Daniel 2:29).
- "Has made known to you what will be" (Daniel 2:29).
- "God has made known to the king what will come to pass after this" (Daniel 2:45).

And the significant event is that the God of heaven will set up a kingdom which will never be destroyed. God's kingdom will consume all other kingdoms and it will stand forever (Daniel 2:44).

Furthermore, the statue is the timeline for when God will establish His everlasting kingdom. The head of gold is Nebuchadnezzar and the Babylonian Empire (Daniel 2:37-38). But his kingdom will pass into another kingdom, one that is lesser in some regards and thus represented by the lesser element of silver. This was the Medo-Persian Empire. In fact, Daniel lived to see this moment come (Daniel 5:30-31).

Yet that empire would not last forever. It would give way to a third empire, an empire "which shall rule over all the earth" (Daniel 2:39). Though its territory is greater than the Babylonians or the Persians, its quality is perceived as lesser, for it is bronze. This was the Grecian Empire, whose zenith was the world conquest of Alexander the Great. Yet this kingdom would not stand forever.

A fourth kingdom is made known by the legs, feet, and toes of the statue. Initially it is iron. The legs crush everything. It breaks in pieces and crushes all other kingdoms. Yet this fourth kingdom cannot last forever. It is fragile because it is divided within itself—iron trying to mix with clay, but "they will not adhere to one another" (Daniel 2:40-43). This fourth kingdom is the Roman Empire. The Roman Empire conquered the world with military might. There was not another world power that consumed them; rather their own inward weaknesses and divisions brought about their demise. This kingdom could not stand forever, either.

And Daniel 2:44 places special emphasis on the Roman Empire: "And in the days of these kings..." At the time of the fourth kingdom—at the time of the Roman Empire—God will establish His kingdom. It begins small but increases and grows to fill the earth. His kingdom consumes all previous kingdoms because it makes citizens of every nation, tribe, and language in the earth. And it stands forever. Long after the demise of the great earthly empires, God's kingdom shall stand glorious and victorious.

Summarizing what we take from Daniel 2 in our equation:

- God will set up a kingdom, and it shall stand forever.
- This will occur in "the latter days"—specifically at the time of the earthly reign of the Roman Empire.
- It will start small, but it will be powerful and grow to consume all kingdoms—it will fill the earth.

Isaiah 2:1-4

Isaiah's prophecy of the establishment of the Lord's house goes hand in hand with the dream of Daniel 2, though it preceded the dream by 150 years or so. Notice that "the mountain of the Lord's house shall be established" in the latter days. Isaiah marks out a similar time period as Daniel (also see Micah 4:1).

Notice that the house shall originate from Zion, the famous hill of Jerusalem. The word of the Lord shall go forth from Jerusalem, and people of all nations (not just Jews) will be drawn or "flow to" it. They will come to the house of the Lord because they desire to be taught His ways and to walk in His paths. And in the established house of the Lord, there will be judgment between nations and many will be rebuked. The way of peace will be made known, and they shall not learn war anymore.

Summarizing what we take from Isaiah 2 in our equation:

- The house of the Lord shall be established.
- This will come to pass in the latter days.
- It originates in Jerusalem.
- The law—the word of the Lord—goes forth from Jerusalem.
- It is for all nations.

Joel 2:28-32

Joel explained that "afterward" (verse 28) and "in those days" (verse 29), God would pour out "My Spirit on all flesh." Here is a sign of the Messianic kingdom: the Holy Spirit is poured out on all nations (Gentiles as well as Jews).

Echoing Isaiah's message, Joel wrote that deliverance will be found in Mount Zion and in Jerusalem because the Lord calls from there (verse 32). From that place, the Lord offers the invitation to salvation, "whoever calls on the name of the Lord shall be saved" (verse 32). Again, we must notice the openness of "whoever"—that means Gentiles and Jews!

Summarizing what we take from Joel 2 in our equation:

- The sign of the Lord: I will pour out My Spirit on all flesh.
- This will come to pass "afterward" and "in those days."
- Salvation is open to all: "whoever calls on the name of the Lord shall be saved."
- The Lord calls from Jerusalem.

Acts 2

With these powerful prophecies before us, we turn our attention to the Acts 2 Pentecost. We learn that:

- The time prophecies were fulfilled. Peter said it was the "last days" (Acts 2:16-17). It was the time of the rule and occupation of the Roman Empire—Daniel's fourth kingdom.
- The location prophecies were fulfilled. The events of Acts 2 occurred in Jerusalem (Acts 1:4, 12; 2:1).
- The sign prophecy was fulfilled. The Lord poured out His Spirit on the apostles and they spoke in tongues (Acts 2:2-4). Peter said this was what Joel prophesied (Acts 2:16-17). A little later in the record, we learn that Gentiles received the same baptism of the Spirit at the house of Cornelius as the apostles at Pentecost (Acts 10:44-48; 11:15-18; 15:7-8).

- The prophesied message was preached. The word of the Lord—salvation for whoever calls on the name of the Lord (Acts 2:21, 36-40).

And so it was the establishment of the kingdom of God. At Pentecost we see that the saved were added to the church (Acts 2:41, 47). People from every tribe and language were there on that day (Acts 2:5-11), and they flowed into the house of the Lord, which is His church (1 Timothy 3:15). Members of His church are those He has transferred into His kingdom (Colossians 1:13).

And the church spread from there. It began in Jerusalem, but the gospel of Jesus Christ went forth into Judea, Samaria, and the end of the earth (Acts 1:8). By the mid 60s A.D., Paul wrote that the gospel was bearing fruit in all the world (Colossians 1:6). The stone grew to a mountain and filled the earth.

Furthermore, where is the Roman Empire? Where is the Babylonian, Persian, or Grecian Empire? These mighty world powers are ancient history. But the kingdom of Christ remains. The church of Christ is here today!

The Kingdom and the Church

The Scriptures show that the Messianic kingdom of prophecy is the New Testament church of Christ.

- Jesus used the words "kingdom" and "church" interchangeably, speaking of the body of people that would be built upon the truth of His identity as Christ and who the apostles would exercise unique authority over (Matthew 16:18-19).

- The kingdom and the church have the same owner: Jesus Christ. "My kingdom" (John 18:36) and "My church" (Matthew 16:18).

- The kingdom and the church have the same ruler: Jesus Christ. He is king of the kingdom (Hebrews 1:8) and head of the church (Colossians 1:18).

- The kingdom and the church have the same beginning place: Jerusalem (Luke 24:47; Acts 2:5; Isaiah 2:2-4).

- The kingdom and the church have the same beginning time: the latter days (Acts 2:16-17; Joel 2:28; Daniel 2:28, 44).

- The kingdom and the church have the same law: the word of God (Isaiah 2:4; 1 Corinthians 9:21; 1 Peter 1:25).

- The kingdom and the church have the same members: Christians (Colossians 1:2, 18; Colossians 1:13).

- The kingdom and the church have the same memorial meal: the Lord's Supper (Matthew 26:26-29; 1 Corinthians 11:20-27).

The New Testament fulfillment of Old Testament prophecy is exciting to study. We see the power of God. We see Him declare through His prophets how events would unfold centuries before they did. And we see that His plan for our redemption was eternally purposed, not a cosmic patch-job to compensate for Jewish disbelief some 2000 years ago.

Christians are a part of something so much bigger than themselves! It's the eternal kingdom of God (Daniel 2:44)! It's the everlasting church of God (Ephesians 3:21)! It is the "Mount Zion," "heavenly Jerusalem," "church of the firstborn," "registered in heaven," "kingdom which cannot be shaken" (Hebrews 12:22-28)! And Christians are a part of it by grace, to serve God acceptably with reverence and fear (Hebrews 12:28).

People don't need to look for the kingdom to come; they need to look to come into His kingdom! They need to "flow to it," as Isaiah wrote. This they can do by the gospel of Jesus Christ. The Lord calls by the gospel (2 Thessalonians 2:14). What was true on Pentecost is true today—"whoever calls on the name of the Lord shall be saved." He will add them to His church; He will make them citizens of His kingdom (Colossians 1:13-14; Revelation 1:5-6).

Lesson 7 Questions

1. What are the consequences for the church, and our understanding of the church, if God's grand scheme was really to establish an earthly kingdom at Christ's first advent all along?

2. When did God conceive of the church?

3. Once the church was established, how long was it to last?

4. What are the benefits of being in the church?

5. How does one get in the church?

6. According to Daniel 2, Isaiah 2, and Joel 2...

    • At what time would the kingdom be established?

    • At what place would the kingdom begin?

- What sign would show the kingdom had come?

- Who would flow into the kingdom?

- What would sound forth from Jerusalem?

7. Now write the verses from Acts 2 that show the fulfillment of all the prophecies listed in question 6.

8. What is the best thing about knowing that the kingdom has come?

9. Why is it difficult for some people to accept that the Messianic kingdom of Old Testament prophecy is the New Testament church of Christ?

10. Do you think some people's understanding of "church" colors their understanding of "kingdom" or vice versa? Explain.

11. What can we do to help others see that Jesus is now reigning as king, that the kingdom prophecies have been fulfilled?

Lesson 8

Prophecy Experts: The Kingdom is Missing

The truth is that Old Testament kingdom prophecy became New Testament church history on the Acts 2 Pentecost. But this truth is rarely heard. The Messianic kingdom of prophecy is the New Testament church of Christ. Yet the modern (and not-so-modern) claims to the contrary are legion. There are acclaimed "prophecy experts" in popular religion today that sell millions of books, CDs, and DVDs on the basic premise that the kingdom has not come—Christ's kingdom is missing!

Their sensational titles, alarming statistics, and ominous predictions have fed what Rod Rutherford called "The Millennial Mania."[36] Such dramatic, "prophetic" works include:

- *The Late Great Planet Earth* by Hal Lindsey
- *On Borrowed Time & 88 Reasons Why the Rapture Will Be in 1988* by Edgar C. Whisenant
- *The End of the Age* by Pat Robertson
- *2001-On the Edge of Eternity* by Jack Van Impe
- *Left Behind* series by Tim LaHaye and Jerry Jenkins

The *Left Behind* series is a popular fiction based on "fact," according to LaHaye. He wrote, "The God who gave me the idea for a work of fiction based on the facts of future Bible prophecy and led me to partner with Jerry has chosen to bless the series beyond our wildest dreams. And the best part of all is that thousands of people have come to faith in Jesus Christ after reading the series…Sold in thirty-seven countries around the world, these books have helped countless believers and unbelievers alike to understand the wonderful plan God has for their future… and the future of all mankind."[37] The books themselves have sold over 65 million copies, and if graphic novels and the *Left Behind: The Kids* series are included, sales exceed 75 million copies.

All of these examples of popular "prophecy experts" are dispensationalists. They contend that the Bible teaches Dispensational Premillennialism as God's "wonderful plan" for the ages, as well as His plan for Christ's kingdom. This lesson introduces the four major views of the Millennial Kingdom of Christ with particular interest in the history and development of Dispensational Premillennialism—the doctrine that prepared such significant numbers of people to consume *Left Behind* products.

Four Views on the Millennium

The word "millennium" comes from two Latin words:

1. "Mille" meaning "thousand"
2. "Annum" meaning "year"

Millennium is commonly used to describe the thousand year reign of Christ mentioned in Revelation 20:1-6. However, since this sole passage in the Bible that mentions such a reign is found in the highly symbolic book of Revelation, there has been much room for speculation as to what it means. Currie frames it well when he writes, "In eschatology, the major point of contention revolves around one issue: the meaning and timing of the Millennium. All Christians agree that the Bible describes a thousand-year reign of Christ. But when does it occur? What is the nature of this reign, corporeal or spiritual? How literal is the thousand years?"[38] Today there are four major schools of thought on this issue.

1. Amillennialism. This is the understanding that the thousand year reign is a figurative number of completeness regarding the blessed state of saints. This view denies that the millennium has literal numerical meaning. This view also denies that after the present dispensation there will be a thousand year reign of Christ on earth.[39] The Messiah is reigning now. His kingdom is spiritual, not earthly.

The prefix "A" is a bit of a misnomer. None deny the millennium outright. Amillennialists deny that it is a physical kingdom, and they also deny that the kingdom is yet to come. Because they believe the kingdom is spiritual and currently established, a better term would be "Realized Millennialism." They believe the millennium is now!

Our study comes from a perspective and interpretation that would be classified Amillennial. The Scriptures bear out the truth that Jesus has reigned over His kingdom since His ascension (Acts 2:30-36; Hebrews 1:8-13; Ephesians 1:20-23). The Messianic kingdom of Old Testament prophecy is the New Testament church of Christ. It may not be the fleshly rule that first century Jews or twenty-first century dispensationalists had in mind, but the lion is the lamb.

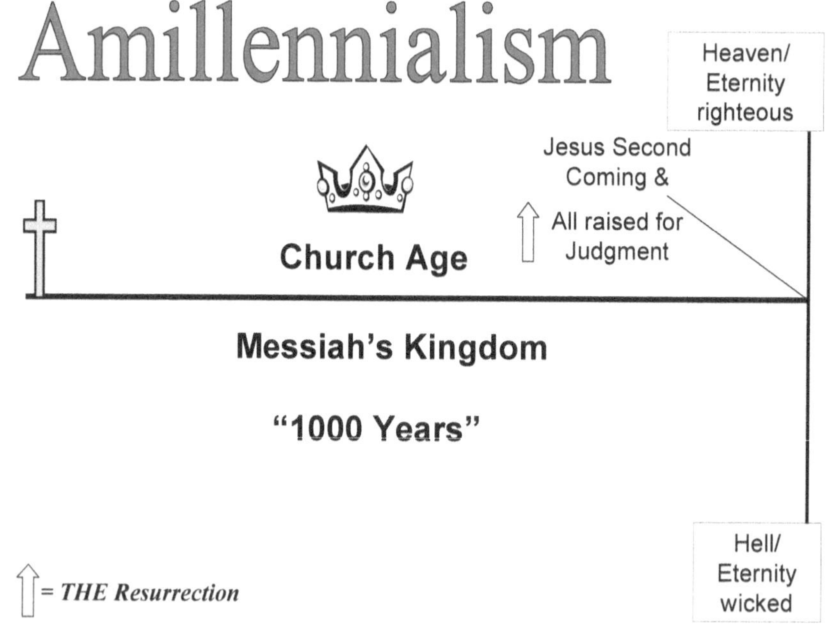

2. Postmillennialism. Postmillennialism is "an optimistic type of theology which predicts a 'golden age,' a Christianized millennium of predominately human achievement before the Second Advent and the subsequent, eternal reign."[40] This interpretation was popularized by Daniel Whitby (1638-1726), a minister in the Church of England.

The central idea of Postmillennialism is that the gospel spreads around the globe with a purifying and renewing effect until the world enters the thousand years of bliss… and then Jesus comes back. In this system, Christianity triumphs over false religion and redeems sinful lives, and as it does, the world gets better and the future gets brighter. Societies develop in the highest principles of men until gradually the world passes into a utopian millennium. Ultimately, Jesus returns for the resurrection and judgment, and souls go to heaven and hell. But Christ's return is after—or Post—the earthly millennium.

Prominent preachers among churches of Christ in the nineteenth century also subscribed to this notion. For instance, Alexander Campbell named his second paper *Millennial Harbinger*, underscoring his conviction that the preaching of the gospel would usher in a literal millennium.

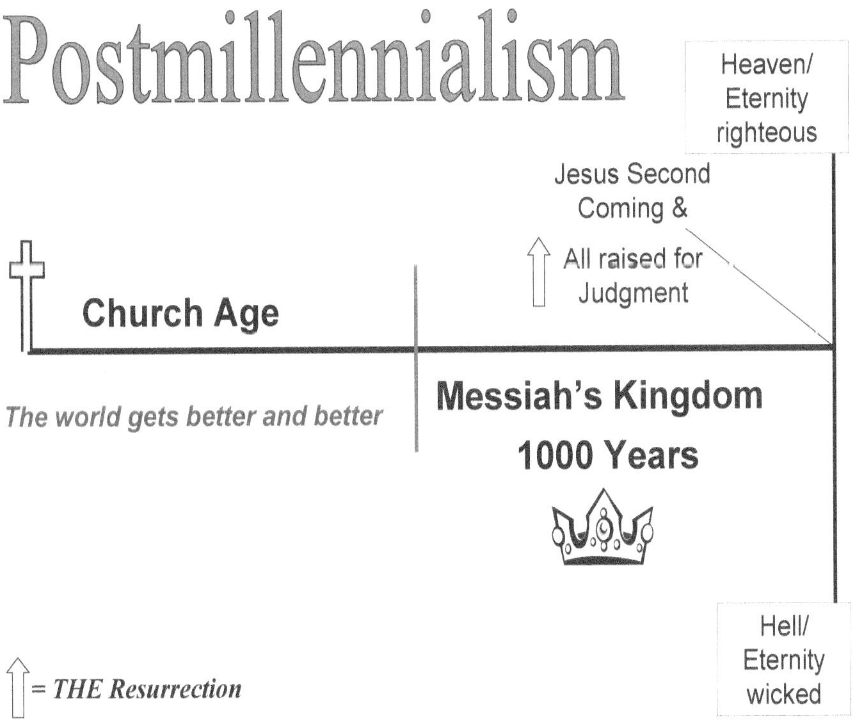

Postmillennialism began to wane (at least in the United States) with the coming of the Civil War. From there the nations witnessed World War I, the Holocaust, and World War II. People rightly doubted the notion that humanity was progressing (by the gospel or any other means) to a utopian millennium before Jesus' Second Coming. Things were not steadily getting better. Evil was not steadily retreating.

3. Historic Premillennialism. There are a variety of understandings of End Times that fall under the category of Premillennialism, a broad system that says Jesus will come back to earth **before** His corporeal kingdom is established and stands for a thousand years. For instance, a particular subset of premillennialists are dispensationalists. All dispensationalists (see below) are premillennialists but not all premillennialists are dispensationalists. In fact, some premillennialists fight very hard against dispensationalism. What are the differences?

George Eldon Ladd identified two major differences in historic premillennialism and dispensationalism. The first difference is in method of interpretation of the Scriptures. Ladd wrote, "Dispensationalism forms its eschatology by a literal interpretation of the Old Testament and then fits the New Testament into it. A nondispensational eschatology forms its theology from the explicit teaching of the New Testament."[41] The second difference is in the area of God's purpose and dealings with the Jews. "The basic premise of Dispensationalism is two purposes of God expressed in the formation of two peoples who maintain their distinction throughout eternity."[42] Historic premillennialists do not hold the position that the church was a Plan B, put in motion because of the Jewish rejection of their Messiah and wholly unforeseen in the Old Testament. They see the church as "spiritual Israel" and believe all men (including Jews) must convert and become Christians to be saved. Conversely dispensationalists hold that God's two peoples (the church and the Jews) must always be distinct, and Jews will be saved ultimately because they are Jews.

Furthermore, typical historic premillennialists believe Jesus will return at the end of the Great Tribulation, while dispensationalists believe Jesus will "rapture" (a secret, silent, snatching away) the church at the beginning of the Great Tribulation.

In the premillennial system, the world gets worse and worse in the church age until Jesus comes, sets up His kingdom, and conquers all the evil.

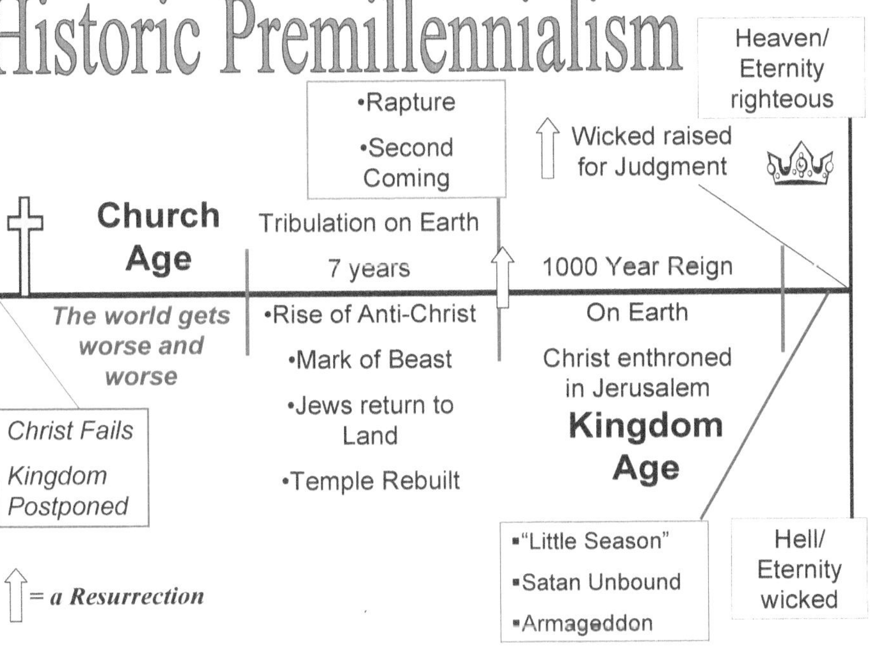

4. Dispensational Premillennialism or Dispensationalism. This is the system popularly preached by Hal Lindsey, Tim LaHaye, and John Hagee (to name a few). The father of dispensationalism is John Nelson Darby (1800-1882), an Anglican priest who rejected his mother church and worked to found the Plymouth Brethren in Great Britain. The whole dispensational system comes about from Darby's two radical presuppositions on the Bible.

First, Darby (and thus dispensationalism) taught that all of human history can be divided into seven successive ages which correspond to the six days of creation and the seventh day of rest:

- The first day = the age of **innocence,** which lasted from creation to the fall.
- The second day – the age of **conscience,** which lasted from the fall to the flood.
- The third day = the age of **human government,** which lasted from the flood to the time of Abraham.
- The fourth day = the age of **promise** which lasted from Abraham to the giving of the Law on Mt. Sinai.
- The fifth day = the age of **law,** which lasted from Sinai to Calvary.
- The sixth day = the age of **grace,** which will last from Calvary to the coming of Christ to establish His kingdom on earth. The church age. This one was unknown in the Old Testament.
- The seventh day = the age of the **kingdom**, which lasts from the second coming of Christ to the end of the millennium when eternity will begin. This should have begun at Christ's first advent but did not.[43]

Second, Darby taught that there were two stories going on in the Bible. As Weber wrote, "To Darby, the Bible revealed two divine plans operating in history, one for an earthly people, Israel, and the other for a heavenly people, the church. Thus, "rightly dividing the word of truth" (2 Tim. 2:15) meant maintaining the distinction between the two peoples of God and never applying biblical passages to one that rightly belonged to the other."[44]

Darby originated the interpretational patchwork of the dispensational system. The trick to it is that he must infallibly determine which scriptures apply to Christianity and which were for Israel and the kingdom. Darby believed that God would not work with His two peoples concurrently. He taught that the church is here because the Jews are gone— dispersed and without their "promised" land. But the kingdom prophecies were for the Jews. So as long as the church is on earth, there cannot be a kingdom. But God prophesied a kingdom in the Old Testament. So Darby preached the Rapture—the secret snatching away of the church by Jesus.

Once the church was out of the way, God could finally do what He always intended: establish the Messianic millennial kingdom for Jews.

As the dispensational system goes, once the church is raptured, the last little bit of salt and light in this world (and the world is ever growing worse and worse) will be gone too. And so dispensationalists draw from symbolic, apocalyptic passages all over the Bible to say literal atrocities are in store for those who are "left behind!" But after seven years of tribulation, Jesus will come back with His saints, deliver Israel at the battle of Armageddon, and establish His literal thousand year kingdom.

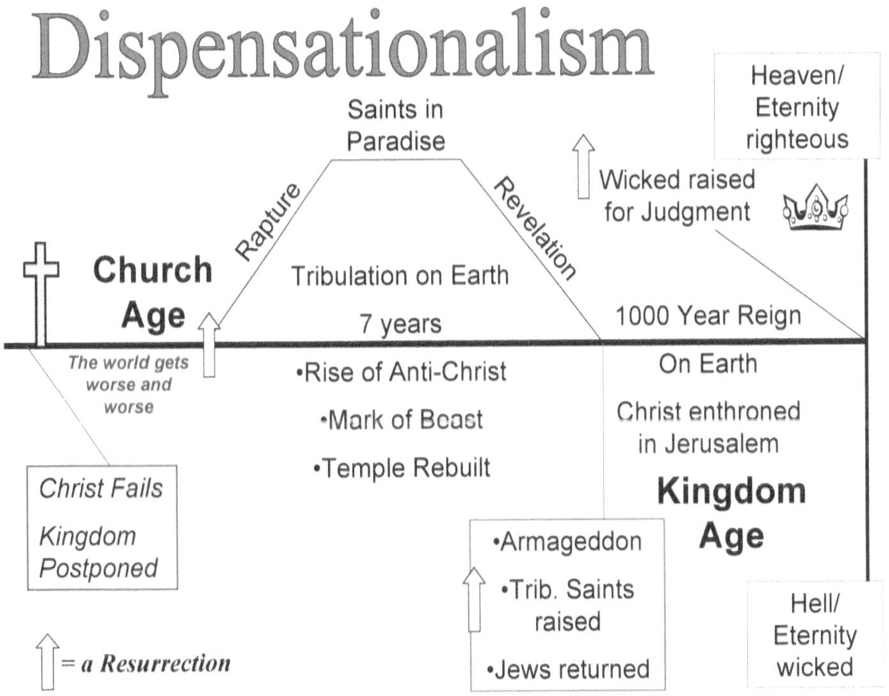

Promoting Dispensationalism

One of the great methods of disseminating dispensationalism throughout the world has been through study Bibles. The great promoter of dispensationalism in the United States was the nineteenth century figure C.I. Scofield, a lawyer and politician who became a minister for the Congregational Church. He powerfully spread dispensatioanlism with two works:

1. *Rightly Dividing the Word of Truth* (1888).
2. *The Scofield Reference Bible* (1908).

While the first book was a theology and defense of dispensationalism, the second actually put dispensational articles, outlines, and references next to the sacred text. Thus the dispensational interpretation was the first commentary people read for the Scriptures. Dispensationalism was the commentary on the page!

This strategy has served dispensationalists well. There is hardly a study Bible on the market today that does not bear the name of a dispensational teacher. Here are six examples:

- C.I. Scofield's *The Scofield Study Bible*
- John MacArthur's *The MacArthur Study Bible*
- Charles Ryrie's *Ryrie Study Bible*
- John Hagee's *The Life Plan Study Bible*
- Tim LaHaye's *Prophecy Study Bible*
- Jack Van Impe's *Jack Van Impe Prophecy Bible*

Surely one can see the impact of linking one Bible verse to the next in reference as if there really is a chain of connection besides the imposition of dispensational doctrine. This cannot help but color the way a new Bible reader understands the kingdom.

Now consider the impact of a century of stadium campaigns, prolific publishing, and even personal study Bibles promoting dispensationalism. Though it is not the historically orthodox understanding of Christ's kingdom, it is the popular understanding of our times.

Yet the common error of postmillennialism, historic premillennialism, and dispensationalism is that Jesus did not establish

His kingdom at His first advent. The bottom line of all these speculative millennial systems is that the kingdom of Christ is missing today!

If It's New, It's Not True

The proponents of all of these millennial positions believe theirs is the one that the Bible actually teaches. Obviously the Bible does not teach all of them. These things are contradictory. So where do modern "prophecy experts" turn to find support? Church history. If the Scriptures taught a position, then surely we'll find believers through the ages that have held it.

Dispensationalists like John Walvoord have made broad historical boasts such as: "Practically all students of the early church agree that premillennialism, or as it is also called, chiliasm, was the view held by many in the apostolic age. It is the oldest of the various millennial views. Chiliasm, from the Greek work *chilias* meaning *one thousand*, is the teaching that Christ will reign on earth for one thousand years following His second advent."[45] Just from reading Irenaeus, one might think that Walvoord is right. Irenaeus wrote about 180 A.D.: "In the times of the kingdom, the earth will be called again by Christ. And Jerusalem will be rebuilt after the pattern of the Jerusalem above."[46]

Also Justin Martyr wrote about 160 A.D.: "I and others who are right-minded Christians on all points are assured that there will be a resurrection of the dead, and a thousand years in Jerusalem, which will then be built... For Isaiah spoke in that manner concerning this period of a thousand years."[47]

However, Walvoord drastically overstates the testimony of the early church. While certain early Christians, like Irenaeus, undeniably wrote things that we would call premillennial today, they were a minority view. Contemporaries of Irenaeus held just the opposite of his future earthly kingdom view. The unknown author of the *Epistle of Barnabas* wrote about 100 A.D.: "For it is written, 'And it shall come to pass, when the week is completed, the temple of God shall be built in glory in the name of the Lord.' I find... that a temple does exist. Having received the forgiveness of sins... in our habitation God dwells in us... This is the spiritual temple built for the Lord."[48]

Even if the seeds of premillennial thought might be found in the writings of Irenaeus or Justin Martyr, it is still a far cry from demonstrating that their doctrine or the doctrine of the early church was dispensationalism. There are significant differences.

The resounding majority of early Christians understood the Messianic kingdom to be spiritual. It had arrived. It was Christ's church. The following quotations are a good sample:

Eusebius quoted Caius who wrote about 215 A.D. "Cerinthus [a heretic], through written revelations by a 'great apostle' (as he would have us believe), brings before us marvelous things – which he pretends were shown to him by angels. He alleges that after the resurrection, the kingdom of Christ is to be on earth and that the flesh dwelling in Jerusalem will again be subject to desires and pleasures."[49]

Origen wrote about 225 A.D. "Certain persons,… adopting a superficial view of the letter of the law,… are of the opinion that the fulfillment of the promises of the future are to be looked for in bodily pleasure and luxury. Therefore, they especially desire after the resurrection to have again bodies that will always have the power of eating, drinking, and performing all the functions of flesh and blood… Consequently, they say that after the resurrection, there will be marriages and the begetting of children. They imagine to themselves that the earthly city of Jerusalem is to be rebuilt, its foundations being laid in precious stones… Moreover, they think that the natives of other countries are to be given them as the servants of their pleasures… They think that they are to receive the wealth of the nations to live on. These views they think to establish on the authority of the prophets, by those promises that are written regarding Jerusalem… And from the New Testament, too, they quote the saying of the Savior … "Henceforth, I will not drink of this cup, until I drink it with you new in My Father's kingdom."… [The millennialists] desire the fulfillment of all things looked for in the promises, all according to the manner of things in this life and in all similar matters… However, those who receive the interpretations of Scripture according to the understanding of the apostles, entertain the hope that the saints will indeed eat – but that it will be the bread of life that can nourish the soul with the food of truth and wisdom."[50]

Finally, Victorinus wrote about 280 A.D. "They are not to be heard who assure themselves that there is to be an earthly reign of a thousand years. They think like the heretic Cerinthus. For the kingdom of Christ is already eternal in the saints – even though the glory of the saints will be manifested after the resurrection."[51]

The early church fathers did not mince words, calling millennial speculations heresy and their promoters heretics. But likely the greatest proof of Ireneaus' erroneous understanding of the millennium was when he set a date for the second coming of Christ.

Irenaeus predicted that the world would end six thousand years after it had begun. He based his calculations on the Bible verse that says that a thousand years is as a day with God (2 Pet. 3:8). "For in as many days as this world was made, in so many thousand years shall it be concluded... In six days created things were completed: it is evident, therefore that they will come to an end at the sixth thousand year"... This means the end of the world would have been around 1000 A.D., although some now claim he meant 2000 A.D. Either way, he was wrong.[52]

Today's "prophecy experts" are declaring the Missing Kingdom! Their erroneous interpretations stand on the shoulders of the convoluted theologians, disgraced date-setters, and false teachers who've gone before them. Their teachings appeal to the carnally minded and they actually rob glory from the reigning King of kings. In the next two lessons we'll look at both spiritual and physical consequences of teaching the Missing Messianic Kingdom.

Lesson 8 Questions

1. Can you think of the last time you heard a person talking about dispensationalism? (They may not have used that word, but they talked about the things that pertain to the system.) Who was it? When was it?

2. Should Christians concern themselves with a fiction, like *Left Behind*? Should we bother with what it says? Why or why not?

3. In your own words…

    What is amillennialism?

    What is postmillennialism?

    What is dispensationalism?

4. Who is the father of dispensationalism?

5. How does dispensationalism differ from historic premillennialism?

6. Who is one of the early Christians that wrote a seemingly premillennial view of Christ's kingdom?

7. What view did other early Christians hold?

8. Who was C.I. Scofield?

9. What did Scofield do to popularize dispensationalism in the United States?

10. How is dispensationalism spread among the public today?

11. What kinds of things should we keep in mind when choosing or reading a study Bible?

12. Name some current, popular dispensational teachers?

Lesson 9

Spiritual Consequences of the Missing Kingdom

Doctrines have consequences. What people are taught informs their beliefs. What people believe motivates their actions. Actions have consequences!

Our last lesson focused on various millennial theories, most of which held that the kingdom of Christ is missing today, but when it comes, it will be a glorious earthly rule and territory. This colors the way people view everyday life and world events. It places one's future hope in carnal things.

This lesson considers the scriptural and spiritual consequences of holding the popular doctrine of dispensationalism. In the next lesson we will consider the temporal consequences of that teaching as it has shaped world events and U.S. foreign policy in the twentieth and twenty-first centuries.

We choose dispensationalism because neither postmillennialism nor historic premillennialism are as feverishly promoted in our time. Your friends may not know the word "dispensationalism," but chances are, they've read *The Late Great Planet Earth* or *Left Behind* or heard John Hagee or Jack Van Impe preach the doctrine on television.

If Dispensationalism Is True, and Christ's Kingdom Is Missing, Then...

The Lord Always Intended to Establish an Earthly Kingdom.
Dispensationalists make the same mistake as first century Jews in expecting their Messiah to establish an earthly kingdom. But Jesus said the kingdom was not with observation (Luke 17:20-21). Jesus said His kingdom was not of this world—it is spiritual (John 18:36-38). The kingdom does not

consist of physical things like eating and drinking (Romans 14:17). People must be spiritually born into it—it is spiritual (John 3:3-5). The Messianic kingdom of prophecy is the church (Matthew 16:16-18). And it has come! It is wrong to teach that Jesus came to establish an earthly kingdom. As Willis wrote, "Jesus did not come in his first coming and will not come in his second coming for the purpose of establishing an earthly kingdom."[53]

The Lord Failed in What He Intended to Do. While dispensationalists hold that God intended for the Messiah to establish an earthly kingdom, they teach that Jesus failed to do this at His first advent. How can God fail? His word is never void, and that includes His word of prophecy (Isaiah 55:10-11). But they say He failed. They teach the kingdom was not established because of Jewish rejection. If this is so, what guarantee is there that Jesus can accomplish this feat at the second coming? He's been stopped before!

This position says terrible things about God! It destroys the omnipotence of God, saying that He failed in His purpose. It destroys the omniscience of God, saying it was not the right time for the establishment of the kingdom, though God thought that it was the right time for the Messiah (Galatians 4:4-5). Jesus said, "the time is fulfilled" (Mark 1:14-15). But we are told He was wrong about that also. Jesus said the kingdom would come in the lifetime of those who saw and heard Him (Mark 9:1). Yet He must have been wrong about that. What blasphemous consequences the doctrine of dispensationalism brings!

Christ's Death on the Cross Was Not Intended As His Purpose. Jesus said He came to seek and save the lost (Luke 19:10). He foretold His death on the cross, as well as His resurrection (Matthew 16:21). He explained the necessity that His blood be shed for the remission of sins (Matthew 26:28). The Scriptures testify that God's plan for the sacrifice of Jesus was made before the creation of the world (Revelation 13:8). The apostles declared the same (Acts 2:23).

But it cannot be both ways. Dispensationalists try to affirm the purpose for the death on the cross when it comes to salvation. But as they teach the kingdom, Jesus died because of the rejection of the Jews, quite unexpectedly—at least in the eyes of Old Testament prophets. Which way is it? Was Jesus crucified as part of God's eternal plan for mankind's salvation, or was Jesus crucified because the Jews rejected their Messiah and their kingdom when He wanted to establish it?

The Church Is an Impromptu Parenthesis in God's Prophetic Plan. As dispensationalists teach it, the church age was only necessary because of the Jewish rejection of Jesus as Messiah—and unforeseen in prophetic scriptures. A 2,000-year gap has occurred between the prophecies that spoke of the coming of the Messiah and the prophecies that spoke of the Messiah establishing His kingdom. Eventually Jesus will return and all the Messianic kingdom prophecies will finally be fulfilled. But Ephesians 3:8-11 declares that the church was part of God's eternal plan. And Jesus Himself spoke of the kingdom in the same breath as the church (Matthew 16:16-18).

There Is Currently No Salvation for Gentiles. According to Acts 15:14-17, "the rest of mankind"—"the Gentiles"—can be saved and be part of the people of God only in David's restored tabernacle. If the Messiah has not yet taken the throne of David, the house of David has yet to be restored to its place of leadership. If the house of David is not restored, then Amos 9:11-12 (which James quoted and said was fulfilled when Peter preached the gospel to the household of Cornelius) is not fulfilled. Gentiles have no opportunity for salvation, and haven't for two millennia! How devastating for all of the Gentile dispensationalists who say Jesus' kingdom still hasn't come! The church age parenthesis isn't really for Gentiles after all.

The Footstool Is Greater than the Throne. In Isaiah 66:1, the prophet makes it clear that heaven is the throne of God and the earth is His footstool. According to dispensationalists, just the opposite is the case. For Jesus is now on His throne in heaven, but this is not good enough for them (Mark 16:19; Hebrews 1:8; Acts 2:30-31). He needs to establish an earthly kingdom. A carnal, millennial kingdom is greater than His present position in the glory of heaven (Ephesians 1:20-23)? Surely not.

There Are Signs That Precede Jesus' Second Coming. Based on their erroneous interpretation of Matthew 24, dispensationalists believe that there are signs that precede the second coming of Jesus Christ. They preach often on the "signs of the times," and believe that the Lord's secret coming of the Rapture is imminent because of world events, political landscapes, and wars. Because of the "signs," prophecy experts have been given to date-setting for Jesus' return throughout the ages (see Appendix). As their dates come and go, they are seen as false prophets, and dispensationalism is debunked; yet, for all the public embarrassment that date-setting has brought, dispensationalism has not gone away!

For instance, Hal Lindsey taught that Jesus must return within forty years of the establishment of the State of Israel in 1948, but 1988 came and went. This date was revised to forty years from 1967 when Jerusalem was returned to Jewish control. But 2007 came and went! No one knows when Christ will come again (Matthew 24:36). He shall come like "a thief in the night" (1 Thessalonians 5:2; 2 Peter 3:10). The signs that Jesus gave in Matthew 24 pertained to the destruction of the Temple and Jerusalem (Matthew 23:37-38; 24:1-3). They were all fulfilled and finished by 70 A.D.

There Are Multiple "Second Comings." Dispensationalists teach that there will be (1) the secret snatching away of the church in the Rapture; (2) Jesus will come with His church to establish the earthly millennial kingdom; (3) Jesus comes in judgment at the end of the 1,000-year reign. That is a lot of "seconds."

But the Bible makes it clear that there was a first coming, when Jesus walked among men, was crucified, buried, and arose. He ascended to heaven, and we are told He will come again for judgment (Acts 1:9-11; 2 Thessalonians 1:6-10). That is a second coming.

There Is a Second Chance for Sinners. While the sensationalistic pitch of dispensationalism is "convert to Christ now, so you won't be left behind," the doctrine actually gives people a false hope for a second chance. As it goes, the church is raptured away, but Bibles and all the writings of rapturists remain. People will continue to learn the gospel and convert. There will be terrible circumstances for the new Christians. They are called Tribulation Saints because the Anti-Christ will bring a horrible persecution—terrible tribulation—upon the new converts. Many of them will be martyred, but they'll be raised up when Jesus comes to establish His earthly kingdom.

Dispensationalists can say that you don't want to be a Tribulation Saint, so don't wait. But in fact, a Tribulation Saint is still spiritually redeemed and delivered from hell! The Bible does not teach a bonus seven years, bad or good, for people to learn the gospel and be saved after Jesus comes. There is one second coming, and if a person is not in Christ when He comes, it is too late (2 Thessalonians 1:8-9; 2 Peter 3:7-13)!

Old Testament Kingdom Prophecies Failed. King Nebuchadnezzar's dream meant that the living God would establish His kingdom during the fourth kingdom, the Roman Empire (Daniel 2:31-44). According to dispensationalists, that did not occur. The kingdom is missing. It is yet future. They claim that there is a 2,000 (and growing)-year gap between the foot and the toes of the image. Once the gap (church age) ends with the Rapture of the church, then the rock can come and smash the toes! Such a presumptuous prophetic parenthesis is preposterous! There is nothing in the book of Daniel or anywhere else in the Bible to suggest that all of Daniel's chronology is off by two millennia unbeknownst to him!

Really, their interpretation looks like a shabby cover-up of failed prophesies. Who can intelligently accept an unknown 2,000-year gap that wasn't revealed until John Nelson Darby? Failed prophecies are false prophecies (Deuteronomy 18:20-22). If the kingdom did not come when God said it would, then it will not come!

The Apostles and New Testament Writers Were Confused. The apostles and early Christians thought the kingdom had come and that they were a part of it. They wrote that the Christians in Colosse were part of the kingdom (Colossians 1:13). The apostle John thought he was in the kingdom (Revelation 1:9). John even wrote that those Christians who'd been redeemed by the blood of Jesus had been made a kingdom of priests (Revelation 1:5-6; 5:9-10). One wonders why Philip and Paul made the kingdom of God such a prominent theme in their preaching (Acts 8:12;

28:30-31) when it did not pertain to anyone they were speaking to, if dispensationalists are correct. How confusing.

These scriptural and spiritual consequences are far too great for any to reasonably subscribe to the doctrine of dispensationalism. It is a terrible error that blasphemes God, twists scripture, and preaches a missing kingdom! It is sensationalistic and ridiculous, and it obscures Christ's glorious kingdom!

Lesson 9 Questions

1. How does a person's understanding of the kingdom (or particular millennial view) change the way they look at and understand the world around them?

2. What kind of kingdom do dispensationalists say Jesus wanted to establish? Did He do that?

3. What is the nature of Christ's kingdom according to His own words?

4. What does it say about the God of the Bible if He, in fact, failed to establish the earthly kingdom when He intended?

5. How do dispensationalists try to preach the crucifixion of Jesus in two different ways? Can both ways be true?

6. What do dispensationalists insert in the Book of Daniel to make their future-kingdom theory work?

7. Who was the first preacher to "find" the church-age gap?

8. Can Gentiles be saved right now if the kingdom has not come? Why or why not?

9. Are there signs that will precede and predict Jesus' second coming? What should we think of those who predict dates for the end of the world?

10. How many "second comings" do dispensationalists teach?

11. Why does the Rapture doctrine actually give sinners a false hope?

12. Should we hope for a kingdom to be established in the future when it did not come on time in the past?

13. What does dispensationalism do to New Testament writers who clearly thought they and other Christians were citizens of Christ's kingdom in the first century?

Carnal Consequences of the Missing Kingdom

Doctrine has consequences! The popular false doctrine of dispensationalism has born terrible fruit. Dispensationalism's missing Messianic kingdom does not merely create a scriptural debacle (as was demonstrated in the last lesson) for Christians. If that was all it achieved, the sheer blasphemy of the teaching would be enough for us to expose it and reject it (Jude 3).

But dispensationalism has placed stumbling blocks before unbelievers. It hinders the cause of Christ, keeping people from faith in Jesus. It creates racism and preaches that God currently has a chosen ethnic group that all other peoples must revere and bless—or suffer judgment. It actively promotes and sustains a national State of Israel through preaching, fundraising, lobbying, and political activism, despite the hardships it brings upon displaced people groups—even Palestinian Christians! Dispensationalism is a false doctrine that has fueled hate, war, and murder in the Middle East over the past sixty years. It is the theological foundation for an earthly State of Israel that predated by at least 100 years the efforts of secular Jews to establish such a nation! It has spawned an entirely anti-Christian movement called "Christian Zionism" to bring about the self-fulfillment of its twisted prophecies and usher in the millennial kingdom.

The Middle East is in turmoil today and a major reason is the false doctrine of dispensationalism. United States foreign policy is unreasonably biased in favor of the State of Israel, and a major reason is the false doctrine of dispensationalism. United States officials cannot be elected president (or other national offices of influence) unless they are pro-Israel, and a major reason is the false doctrine of dispensationalism.

Many sincere Bible believers have been misled by dispensationalism and the false prophets that aggressively promote it. But those who try to clear the Bible's name by setting the record straight on dispensationalism and Christian Zionism are defamed as genocidal anti-Semites. Franklin Littell's words illustrate this well:

> The cornerstone of Christian anti-Semitism is the superseding or displacement myth, which already rings with the genocidal note. This is the myth that the mission of the Jewish people was finished with the coming of Jesus Christ, that "the old Israel" was written off with the appearance of "the new Israel." To teach that a people's mission in God's providence is finished, that they have been relegated to the limbo of history, has murderous implication which murderers will in time spell out.[54]

Also, John Hagee wrote:

> Some evangelicals teach that God has replaced Israel. This is an anti-Semitic theology that refuses to believe God still has a place in His heart for Israel and the Jewish people.[55]

According to them, teaching that the Messiah has fulfilled the Law and prophets is anti-Semitic (Matthew 5:17-18)? Saying that the kingdom has come and that God's nation is a spiritual nation composed of every race as opposed to a single ethnicity is murderous (Colossians 1:13-14; 3:11; Galatians 3:26-29)? Proclaiming that there is one way of salvation for Jew and Greek through Christ's church is to become a murderer (Romans 1:16; 10:12; Ephesians 2:14-16)?

Such slurs may intimidate truth seekers from questioning—let alone challenging—dispensationalism or the Zionist agenda. But it is nothing new for Christians to be reviled falsely for Christ's sake (Matthew 5:11).

Anti-Semitism is wrong, but not because Jews are currently God's earthly nation. Anti-Semitism is wrong because the New Testament condemns bigotry and racial prejudice of any kind. Ironically, the passages that condemn racism are more often than not directed toward Jews who had a difficult time accepting Gentiles as equals in the eyes of God (Acts 10:9-16, 28, 34-35; 11:1-18; 15:1-31; Romans 2:28-29; Galatians 3:7-9; Ephesians 2:11-18). Nevertheless, it is equally wrong for Gentiles to hate other Gentiles or Jews.

The immediate physical consequences of dispensationalism laid forth here do call into question a biblical case for Zionism. Yet this does not come from any prejudice or anti-Semitism. There may be legitimate reasons for a State of Israel to continue in Palestine. But let neither God nor the Bible be charged for its current existence and state of affairs. Ours is a deep concern that all men know the redemptive truth of God's word (1 Timothy 2:1-4). However, that truth is terribly obscured from many people because of the carnal consequences of dispensationalism.

If Dispensationalism Is True, and Christ's Kingdom Is Missing, Then...

Skepticism is Fueled

The apostle Peter warned that Scripture could be twisted by unstable people, and this would bring about destruction (2 Peter 3:16). Today, self-proclaimed "Prophecy Experts" are preaching wild speculation, paranoid delusion, and sensational scenarios of the coming End of Days. But what makes these dispensationalists especially destructive is that they try to cite Scripture for all of it. And if the meaning of prophetic scripture can be revised and reinterpreted so many times, then it looks to the world as if it has no meaning at all. Their teachings are rich fodder for skeptics!

An example of this would be the *Jack Van Impe Presents* broadcast. According to the website: "'Jack Van Impe Presents' is a weekly news program which analyzes and evaluates world events in the light of biblical prophecy. Dr. Jack Van Impe and Rexella Van Impe report and interpret international news."[56] This television show features Dr. Van Impe and his wife Rexella sitting together at an evening-news-style desk. Rexella reads headlines collected from all over the world and says, "What about it, Jack?" Then Jack mentions a few scriptures, rarely taking the time to quote a phrase from more than one of them, and says something to the effect of, "it's all happening just as the Bible foretold." Yet he quotes incessantly from the same texts! How can a single text refer to an endless list of events?

Biblical Christianity and the credibility of the Bible itself suffer because false teachers try to tie their predictions to it. Then when things do not occur as "foretold," people charge the Bible with error instead of the teachers. Many are aware that dispensational doctrine is embarrassing to the cause of Christ. Professor and author Paul L. Maier wrote:

> Throughout the history of the Christian church, wrongheaded teachings have appeared that temporarily attracted a large following, only to become fading fads once the light of proper biblical interpretation illuminated their error. A current example is the dispensational, pretribulational-rapture theology promoted by such prophecy pundits as Hal Lindsey, Tim LaHaye, John Walvoord, Thomas Ice, John Hagee, and others. For years now, I've been wondering what might convince such prophecy specialists to recognize that the eschatology they are foisting on the world is simply embarrassing to the church, and so prompt them to back out of their dispensational cul-de-sac.[57]

Jesus' woes upon the Pharisees of His day fall with equal weight upon modern dispensational "prophecy experts." It is the dispensationalists that travel far and wide, feverishly promoting their religious system seeking to make proselytes. But the end result is that their prophecy-proselytes are further from God now than they were before (Matthew 23:15). Dispensationalism keeps people out of Christ's kingdom because it denies it has come, and these false teachers certainly are not entering in on their present course (Matthew 23:13)!

The more books these Bible "literalists" write—the more dates they set that pass by without Christ's Coming (see Appendix)—the more microchip-mark-of-the-beast fantasies they concoct—the more the world shakes its head with renewed skepticism and disbelief.

Racism Is Reasonable

Dispensationalism holds that God has two peoples. He has the earthly people of Israel, and He has the spiritual people that are His church, composed of mainly Gentiles. This distinction of plans and peoples that Darby postulated in his dispensational doctrine is an important division between dispensationalists and historic premillennialists. In the nineteenth century, both doctrines held that the Jews must return to their land in order that Jesus might eventually reign in His kingdom. But Sizer noted:

> As the postmillennialism of the Reformation and Puritanism gave way to a more pessimistic premillennialism of the early nineteenth century, two differing views regarding the relationship of the church to the Jewish people emerged at the same time and developed in parallel. Historic or covenantal premillennialism believed that the Jewish people would be incorporated within the church and return to Palestine a converted nation alongside other Christian nations. Dispensational premillennialism, however, came to believe the Jewish people would return to the land before or after their conversion but would remain distinctly separate from the church.[58]

Dispensationalism—with its racial discrimination—was controversial from the beginning of Darby's movement. Benjamin Newton (1807-1899) was a close associate of Darby and fellow minister among the Plymouth Brethren. While he initially accepted Darby's dispensational understanding of premillennialism, he ultimately rejected major tenants, including the Rapture and the position on earthly Israel. "Newton eventually came to recognize Darby's elevation of Israel above the church as heresy, and repudiated the idea that the Jews could be blessed apart from faith in Jesus Christ. It was 'virtually to say there are two kinds of Christianity, two Gospels, two ways, and two ends of salvation.'"[59]

Dispensationalism says that God has an earthly race: the Jews. And this race needs to be treated especially well so that Gentile nations can be blessed and escape God's wrath. Dispensationalists turn to God's promise to Abraham—"I will bless those who bless you, and I will curse him who curses you"—and make blanket application to all his ethnic descendants through Isaac as well as the national State of Israel today. And that is racism. They teach that Jews are inherently better, protected by God, and blessed by men because of their race.

The applications can be quite frightening for those peoples' interests that conflict with the interests of Jews. In the twentieth century, indigenous Palestinians were pushed off their lands beginning in 1917 with a Jewish immigration movement. Palestinian leaders tried to work peacefully through the 1) British Government (the colonial ruler of Palestine following the dismantling of the Ottoman Empire), then 2) League of Nations, and later 3) the United Nations to protest the influx of Jews that were (in some cases) militantly removing Palestinians from their property. Yet the "Christianized" world powers would not take up for the Palestinians in any meaningful way. For a time Great Britain attempted to enforce its immigration policy, limiting Jewish settlers to 5,000 a year. But Jews in Palestine organized the *Irgun* (Israeli guerilla fighters and terrorists) to attack British forces, stop deportations, and dominate Palestinians. The end result is that today, Palestinians form the largest displaced people group in the world.[60]

Today, popular opinion tends to blame the Palestinians for the violence and turmoil in the Middle East. But in fact, Palestinians tried to work through peaceful measures for thirty years, only to see the State of Israel declared in 1948! As Jews moved in and the State expanded, Palestinians were pushed off their lands and didn't have anywhere to go!

Dispensationalism fed the racism that empowered the establishment of the State of Israel. The doctrine said that Jews are God's earthly people and Gentiles better help the cause of Israel. It viewed Palestinians as a lesser people fighting Israel over land. In fact, some dispensationalists today go so far as to deny that Palestinians are even a people! They act like Palestinians have not lived in Palestine for the past 2,000 years and more! William Baker helps us see who Palestinians are:

> Please note that the land called "Palestine" was
> occupied long before the emergence of any nation or group

called "Hebrews." The name Palestine is the oldest name of the country, and is called 'pelesheth' in Hebrew, and 'phylistieim' in Greek. Both refer to the original inhabitants of the land, the Philistines, hence the name of the land was called Palestine, meaning "the land of the Philistines."… One must realize that the ancestors of the great majority of the Arabs of Palestine did not enter Palestine with the Moslem invasion. In fact, Palestinians are primarily descendants of those Semites who occupied Palestine from time immemorial, namely, the Canaanites and other Semitic tribes, and of the Jews who were taken into captivity by the Assyrians or the Babylonians, and ultimately absorbed by the remainder of the population. Naturally, they also include the descendants of those non-Semites who may have remained behind after the Persians, Macedonians, Romans and other conquerors had been driven out by the Arab invasion, and who were completely Arabised by that invasion. This applies to the remnants of subsequent invaders including the Crusaders.[61]

Palestinian is its own race, and the history of that people is closely intertwined with the Middle East region still called Palestine. Today, most Palestinians are Muslim, but there are also Christian and Jewish Palestinian minorities. The West has and does favor the Jewish interest over the Palestinian interest. One factor for this is the dispensational belief that to work against the State of Israel is to work against God's earthly nation. And Bible believers understand that you cannot fight against God (Acts 5:38-39). Thus many come down on Israel's side.

Where do self-professed Christians turn in the New Testament to get the idea that God has a preferred earthly nation today? No passage teaches it. But an unscrupulous handling of Scripture, along with the common dispensational practice of forcing their system onto the Bible, will provide a few passages. An example of convenient and suspect dispensational scholarship comes from John Hagee. He contends that if you divorce three chapters from the middle of the book of Romans as a "stand-alone document," it teaches that God still has an earthly race: Israel.

Romans 9-11 is a magnificent theological codicil, which is a stand-alone document. When a lawyer makes a will, then remembers there is something he wishes to add into the will after it has been written, the portion added is a codicil. The codicil modifies the original document and becomes part of the whole. Romans 9-11 is a divine codicil by Saint Paul concerning God's post-Calvary position on the Jewish people... Romans 9-11 is a theological codicil, which makes it a stand-alone document... it is instantly obvious that chapters 9, 10, and 11 have nothing to do whatsoever with chapters 1 through 8 or 12 through 16... The fact is that Romans 9-11 is a stand-alone document and represents God's post-Calvary position paper on the Jewish people.[62]

This is the most thinly veiled effort at proof-texting and Scripture twisting imaginable. To take modern practices of jurisprudence and legalese and foist them onto a 2,000-year-old letter is quite the stretch! You cannot take a letter—no matter how much argumentation it may contain—and parse it like a will or other contract. They are distinct types of literature with distinct principles of interpretation. Hagee is so desperate to find evidence of God holding onto an ethnic race that he asserts "chapters 9, 10, and 11 have nothing to do whatsoever with chapters 1 through 8 or 12 through 16." What presumption!

Yet even his codicil theory does not say what he needs it to. Right in the middle of God's supposed "position on the Jewish people" we read:

"For there is no distinction between Jew and Greek, for the same Lord over all is rich to all who call upon Him," (Romans 10:12).

Hagee says these three chapters—when kept completely separate from all that precedes and follows in the book of Romans—prove there is a distinction for the Jews. But Paul wrote that there is no distinction!

And why would there be? God has fulfilled His purpose and all promises regarding the biblical people of Israel. He is done with having a physical nation.

- God made a promise to Abraham about Canaan, and He fulfilled that word—Israel received the Promised Land (Genesis 15:18; Joshua 21:43-45; 2 Chronicles 9:26).
- Furthermore, God made a covenant with Israel about keeping the land. Keeping the land was conditional (Joshua 23:14-16). Israel did not respect the covenant they entered into with God. He kept His word, and they lost the land.
- God promised that He would bring back a remnant to the land, and He kept His word (Jeremiah 23:7-8; 2 Chronicles 36:22-23).
- Finally, there are no New Testament prophecies that say Israel must be re-gathered to Canaan or that God will give them Canaan… again.

For what purpose does God require an earthly nation? Physical Israel doesn't hold anything necessitating God's restoration of it:

- God has a temple, His church (1 Corinthians 3:16; Ephesians 2:21-22). So He doesn't want Jerusalem.
- God has a house, His church (1 Timothy 3:15). So He doesn't want Jerusalem.
- God has a people, His church (1 Peter 2:9-10). And Jews are invited to be a part. In fact, Paul laments that so many refused the gospel and fellowship as God's people (Romans 9:1-5; 10:1-4). But the gospel was for them first (Romans 1:16). Any—Jew or Greek—can be part of God's spiritual nation today.
- God does not need Jerusalem to be worshipped (John 4:21, 23-24).

God's purpose for the Israelite race from the very beginning was to have a separate people to bring the Messiah into the world for the benefit of all nations (Genesis 22:18). God accomplished this in Jesus Christ and has no other special plan for earthly Israel revealed in the Bible (Romans 9:3-5). Christ is the culmination!

Today there is only one plan of redemption for all races. There is not one plan for the Jewish race and another for all the Gentiles (Romans 1:16; Galatians 1:6-9; Acts 15:11). This is denied by dispensationalists today who say God will make a way to save all of Israel regardless of their choice or the gospel. But the New Testament makes it clear that God is not a respecter of persons, and no one will be saved on the basis of their DNA (Romans 10:12). God does not have an earthly race today. But dispensationalists twist the Scripture to say that He does, and so racism becomes reasonable, even scriptural.

Zionism Is Mandated

According to the World Zionist Organization (a Jewish political group), "Zionism seeks to secure for the Jewish people a publicly recognized, legally secured home in Palestine." Premillennialists are on board with this. They differ over whether the Jews must be converted to Christ. Historic premillennialism's view was that the Jews would mass convert, return to Palestine, and usher in Jesus' earthly millennial kingdom. Dispensationalists said that the Jews get to have Canaan back because God promised Abraham He would give them the land forever. At issue is whether Christians need to evangelize Jews along with their efforts to support the national State of Israel.

If there is genuine concern about working against the purposes of God, perhaps a good question to consider is how Jews came to be displaced and dispersed at all? In fact, the Bible shows that the *Diaspora* is the fulfillment of prophecy. It was the will of God. God's judgment dispersed them from Canaan in A.D. 70, and made a restoration of the ancient nation of Israel impossible.

How long was biblical Israel a united, independent State? Actually it was only a sovereign power for about eighty years. Isn't that curious? It was hardly consolidated under the rule of King Saul. He spent his time (when not chasing David) fighting for independence and territory against Ammonites, Amalekites, and Philistines. When he obeyed God, he won, and when he rebelled from God, he lost. But Israel was hardly "settled" as a State during his reign.

Certainly from David's rule in 1000 B.C. through Solomon's rule it was united, powerful, peaceful, and prosperous. But then the kingdom divided when Rehoboam came to power. The two southern tribes of Judah and Benjamin became the kingdom of Judah, and the ten northern tribes became the kingdom of Israel.

Let's notice that in the scope of all human history, a span of eighty years—less than one century—is the "glory days" of a kingdom, a national state called Israel. And there are a couple of reasons for this. First, God's plan was never to have a physical nation ruling the earth. He wanted a physical nation through which to bring a Messiah to save all the nations of the earth. Second, God wasn't pleased about Israel demanding a king (1 Samuel 8:7; Hosea 13:9-11). In fact, God takes credit in the Book of Hosea for providing and removing Israel's monarchy and national sovereignty (Hosea 13:9-11).

Jesus prophesied the destruction of Jerusalem (Luke 19:41-44; 21:5-6, 20-24; 23:28-31). His words are recorded in all three of the Synoptic Gospels. In A.D. 70, God exercised judgment on the Jews through the Roman generals of Vespesian and Titus.

Jerusalem's destruction in 70 A.D. was complete, and it made the rebirth of biblical Israel impossible. Here is why:

- The Temple was destroyed – no temple worship, no true practice of the Law of Moses. The acceptance and practice of the Law of Moses was essential to their identity.
- The Genealogies were lost – no tracing families for land rights or to have Levites. There can be no priests or kings for Israel.
- The people were scattered and intermarried – there is no such thing as a pure-blooded Jew today as existed before 70 AD. No one can demonstrate that he or she is a direct descendent of Abraham. In all likelihood, no such bloodline exists at all. Some of the Jews who remained in the aftermath of the Roman destruction intermarried Palestinians, and their descendants are the Palestinians being forced out of Palestine today for an Israeli State.

God dispersed the Jews and made the restoration of biblical Israel impossible. And so there was no Jewish state and very little Jewish presence to speak of in Palestine from 70 A.D. until the early twentieth century. God dispersed the Jews according to the prophecies of Jesus—and He did it quite thoroughly. And there are no prophecies after Jesus that say the Jews will be restored.

Yet there is a State of Israel in Palestine, and it has been there since 1948. It is populated with people who claim to be Jews. How did that come to pass? Dispensationalists say it was a miracle. Hagee wrote, "The greatest prophetic miracle of the twentieth century [was] the rebirth of the State of Israel, May 14, 1948, at 4:32 p.m."[63] But the establishment of the State of Israel was not "prophetic." No New Testament prophecies were fulfilled by its creation. It was not a "miracle." Far from supernaturally and inexplicably occurring, the State of Israel declared its existence through the legal channels and backing of the United Nations. And the establishment of the State of Israel was not a "rebirth," or restoration of biblical Israel. We have already noticed that with no Temple and no genealogies, there can be no priests, no kings, and no adherence to the Law of Moses.

Theodore Herzl

Instead we need to learn about a secular Jewish man and his movement: Political Zionism. Theodore Herzl (1860-1904) is credited with being the father of Zionism and the founder of the Zionist movement.

Herzl was a Jew born in Budapest, Hungary, in 1860. In 1884, he and his family moved to Vienna where Herzl earned a law degree. By 1892, Herzl worked as the French correspondent for the large Vienna newspaper, *Neue Freie Presse*.

In 1894, while on assignment in Paris, Herzl covered the trial of an army captain named Alfred Dreyfus. Dreyfus was the sole Jewish member of the French Army General Staff. He was accused of spying for Germany. Because of the nature of the charges, the trial was confidential, and press could only attend the opening session for charges and the closing session of the verdict. Herzl attended both. He was struck by the genuine tone of Dreyfus' cries, "I am innocent." But the court found Dreyfus guilty. He was degraded from his rank. As Dreyfus was carried off, the crowd in the courtroom began to shout, "Death to the Jews." Herzl was deeply moved by the hate and anti-Semitism. That moment shaped the rest of his life's work.

Immediately Herzl began to consider the plight of Jews all over Europe. They had failed to assimilate in their European homes. They were subject to the discrimination, prejudice, and persecutions of anti-Semitism. He felt he must resolve the "Jewish question." So in 1896, Herzl wrote *The Jewish State*, a manifesto that addressed the difficulties of Jews in Europe and answered that they need to work politically to get their own country.

In 1897, Herzl organized 200 Jewish delegates in Basel, Switzerland, for the purpose of founding the World Zionist Organization (W.Z.O.). This group of wealthy, influential, politically connected Jews and Zionist sympathizers set about the task of establishing a State of Israel in Palestine. Herzl wrote in his diary, "Were I to sum up the Basel Congress in a word—which I shall guard against pronouncing publicly—it would be this: at Basel I founded the Jewish State. If I said this aloud today, I would be answered by universal laughter. Perhaps in five years, and certainly in fifty, everyone will agree." Fifty-one years after penning those words, in May of 1948, the modern State of Israel declared independence.

The World Zionist Organization defined their cause strictly as securing a state for the Jewish people in Palestine. They would not compromise concerning Palestine. In 1903, Herzl had worked out a deal with the British government, who offered Uganda to the World Zionist Organization as land for a Jewish State. Herzl was excited for the plan, but the W.Z.O. rejected it, and Herzl was disappointed. He was not especially religious—he simply believed Jews in Europe needed their own land. Most Zionists (Jews and premillennialists alike) determined that the land had to be Palestine.

Zionism Timeline 1896-1948
- 1896 – Theodor Herzl publishes *The Jewish State*.
- 1897 – Formation of the World Zionist Organization (W.Z.O.). This is the first and main body that works with European nations toward establishing a Jewish State in Palestine.
- 1903 – Britain offers W.Z.O. Uganda, but they refuse it.

- 1917 – Ottoman Empire dissolves at the close of WWI, and Britain controls Palestine.
- 1917 – *Balfour Declaration*. Some British officials think it's good for Jews to have Palestine as a homeland. This allows limited immigration of European Jews into Palestine.
- 1922 – *British White Paper*. Palestinians are upset at the numbers of Jews immigrating and feel themselves being overrun. They allege that the Jews intend to have a Jewish nation. Britain clarifies in this document that that is not their goal. They want Jews and Palestinians to live together. This document seeks to appease Palestinian concerns and restricts the number of Jewish immigrants to 5,000 per year.
- 1922 – *The Palestine Mandate* by The League of Nations. The League institutes a Mandatory, a type of governing agency to help the British smooth the tensions between native Palestinians and immigrating Jews. There are concerns that the well-financed Jews are buying up all the land, forcing Palestinians off their lands, and taking over jobs and the economy. But Jewish immigration continues and is encouraged.
    - o Jews continue to immigrate to Palestine at a slow rate, until Hitler comes to power. Once Hitler's agenda is known among European Jews, many flee for Palestine.
    - o Great Britain strictly enforces their immigration policy, and illegal Jewish immigrants are captured and sent back to their nation of origin—usually back to countries controlled by Nazis.
    - o During this time, the *Irgun* is organized. These are Israeli guerilla fighters who attack British troops and targets that are involved in deporting illegal immigrant Jews.
- 1947 – *United Nations General Assembly Resolution 181*. The allies agree that reparations must be made to the Jews for the Holocaust. Jews should have the state that Zionists have been striving to achieve for fifty years. They decree that a joint government of Jews and Palestinians should be established. But really they divide the land and give X number of acres for Jewish settlement and X number of acres for the indigenous Palestinians to live on. The end result is that Palestinians are displaced.

- 1948 – *Declaration of Israel's Independence.* Britain relinquishes control of a portion of Palestine to a government of the Israeli State. Israel is embroiled in military struggle with the Palestinians at this point who do not want there to be an Israeli government in their land. In fact, they have been protesting and working with Britain to avoid such a government for fifty years. To no avail. The Palestinians lose the battles.

This is all hardly miraculous. Historical facts should be recalled when dispensationalists suggest God worked a miracle in establishing the State of Israel in 1948. This was not God leading Israel out of Egypt all over again. Furthermore, the modern State of Israel distanced herself from the God of the Bible.

Fact - The phrase "God of Israel" was struck from the Declaration of Israel's Independence so as not to offend Jewish secularists. It was replaced with "Rock of Israel."

Fact - The authority of Yahweh was never cited in the Declaration of Israel's Independence; instead, the declaration reads, "by virtue of the natural and historic right of the Jewish people and the Resolution of the General Assembly of the United Nations, we hereby proclaim the establishment of the Jewish state in Palestine."

- They said they could exist because of a natural right of the Jewish people.
- They said they could exist because of a historic right of Jewish people.
- They said they could exist because the United Nations said they could.
- But they said nothing about God's decree or fulfilled prophesy or anything of that nature.

Fact - From the declaration of 1948, The State of Israel has existed as a national body, but not a theocracy. They gave no credit to any god.

Let's compare the biblical Israel with the modern State of Israel to see if God restored them in 1948.

Bible Israel	State of Israel (1948)
Monarchy	Democratic Republic
Theocracy	Religious Freedom
Law of Moses	Modern Jurisprudence
Pure Bloodline	No Genealogies
Given Land	Disputed Territory
Hebrew Language	Diverse Languages
Temple Worship	Wailing Wall

It is obvious that the accomplishment of the Zionist movement is in no way a restoration or revival of biblical Israel. It can hardly be called an act of God when no prophecy has been fulfilled and no miracle has been witnessed. This State came about as all other worldly nations—through diplomacy, political power plays, and military victory. Today, the State of Israel tries to control portions of disputed territory. But they struggle to control it, and there is no peace because God did not give this land to them, they took it.

What's so Christian about Christian Zionism?

Dispensationalists preach today that a Christian's responsibility is to support the State of Israel. They lobby politicians to make sure that the United States continues to back Israel in the region and send billions of dollars in support to it annually. They raise funds among Christians to help Jews from all over the world move to Israel. And they do it because they believe modern Israel is God's people who will finally enjoy the Messiah's kingdom. They teach that the missing kingdom will finally appear soon.

John Hagee addressed the American Israel Public Affairs Committee (AIPAC), the largest Israel Lobby group in the United States, and said, "I want to say this as clearly and plainly as I possibly can: Israel, you are not alone. Ladies and gentlemen, it's a new day in America. The sleeping giant of Christian Zionism has awakened. Fifty million Christians are standing up and applauding the State of Israel."[64]

If there really is such a giant as Christian Zionism, it is surely a Goliath that needs to be slain by the truth of the Word of God. How could any teaching that twists the Scriptures as dispensationalism does be from God? It is not biblical. And if this system is not biblical, then there is no biblical foundation for the Zionist movement. And if there is no biblical foundation for the Zionist movement, then Christians had better flee from it and cease promoting the lie that the modern State of Israel is the product of a miracle.

What should be a Christian's perspective on the State of Israel? It is a mission field (Mark 16:15-16)! All who live there need the gospel. The Jews need the gospel of Jesus Christ (Romans 1:16; 9:1-5; 10:12) as well as the Palestinians and Muslims (Romans 1:16).

But regardless of their future existence as a sovereign state—whether the current political State of Israel succeeds or fails—it will neither hasten nor pause the return of Jesus Christ and the end of the world. The kingdom is not missing. His kingdom has come.

Lesson 10 Questions

1. How can you answer a skeptic who wants to lump you in with the Jack Van Impe, Tim LaHaye, End Times Christians?

2. How can you answer a skeptic who says, "You Christians can't even agree on what the Bible says yourselves, why should I do what it says"?

3. How does dispensationalism actually promote racism?

4. Why do dispensationalists actively support (politically, financially) the State of Israel?

5. How do dispensationalists guard against anyone questioning or challenging Zionism?

6. Who is the father of Zionism?

7. What event put Herzl on the course of establishing the Zionist movement?

8. Was the State of Israel that came into existence in 1948 a restored biblical Israel? Why or why not?

9. Can Zionism be questioned without it being anti-Semitic?

10. How can Christians show love to Jews without involving the church in Zionism?

11. How can Christians show love to Palestinians without being anti-Semitic?

12. Do you think there is a giant of Christian Zionism waking up in our land? Why or why not?

13. How can we challenge proud "Christian Zionists" in the United States?

A Pride of Lambs:
The Kingdom That Doesn't Look Like a Kingdom

The lion is the lamb! Though Jesus certainly is the Messiah, the Lord of lords and King of kings, He did not appear to be an earthly king. The great victory of the lion-ruler was in the lowly defeat of the lamb-sacrificed. His death upon the cross paid the price of sin. His resurrection broke the bondage of death. Forgiveness and the promise of everlasting life in heaven can only be found in Him.

Undoubtedly, the Jews of Jesus' day wanted an earthly king. In fact, for a time, they wanted Jesus to be that king (John 6:15). Crowds lauded Him as the prophesied "Son of David"—a Messianic title communicating a warrior-king to deliver them from the oppression of earthly enemies and restore David's kingdom (Matthew 21:9; Mark 11:9-10).

Jesus was the promised descendant of David (Acts 13:22-23). And He came to establish a kingdom. But it was not a corporeal kingdom tied to the territory of Palestine. His kingdom is spiritual, worldwide, and eternal. His rule encompasses all nations.

Jesus was a warrior-king par excellence. But His enemies were not Roman legions. His was a mission of salvation, and His enemies were all the wicked forces and sin that kept souls in bondage. He has triumphed over spiritual enemies (Colossians 1:15). He has slain the dragon—destroyed the devil and his power (Hebrews 2:14-15). And a day is coming in which all the physical universe that seems to obscure Christ's ultimate preeminence from so many mortal eyes shall be shaken and removed by fire, and every tongue will confess that Jesus is Lord (Hebrews 12:25-29; 2 Peter 3:7, 10-12; Philippians 2:9-11).

The king has a kingdom. The Messianic kingdom of Old Testament prophecy is the New Testament church of Christ.

This lesson explores two things: first, there are parallels between Christ's kingdom and earthly kingdoms. These help us see the truth that a spiritual kingdom is no less real. Second, it must be observed that just as Jesus did not meet the popular expectation of the king, so too, His kingdom doesn't match corporeal expectations either. Particular differences between Christ's kingdom and earthly kingdoms will be highlighted.

Four Things Constitute a Kingdom

Let's begin with the parallels that help us see that Christ, in fact, has a kingdom today. What is necessary to constitute a kingdom? Four things constitute a kingdom: king, subjects, law, and territory.

1. A King

We have already observed that the primary meaning of both the Hebrew and Greek words translated "kingdom" in our English Bibles is exercised authority or rule. Only secondarily does it communicate territory. The logical application to territory follows because of the recognition of rule. This being understood, the first thing needed for a kingdom is a king: that one who rules and exercises authority. The king is Jesus Christ the Lord (Matthew 28:18).

Consider Jeremiah 23:5-6. There it is prophesied that the Lord "will raise to David a Branch of righteousness; a King shall reign and prosper and execute judgment and righteousness in the earth." He would have authority over Judah and Israel—the Jews and the house of Jacob. In the New Testament we learn that this descendant king of David is Jesus Christ. Read Luke 1:31-33 and Matthew 2:2.

Consider Isaiah 9:6-7. There it is prophesied that the "Son" will be placed "Upon the throne of David and over His kingdom… from that time forward, even forever." The child that is born, the son that is given, is Jesus Christ! In the New Testament we learn that the son did ascend to the throne of David. Read Luke 1:31-33 and Acts 2:22-36.

Consider Zechariah 6:12-13. There it is prophesied that the "Branch" will "build the temple of the Lord" and He "shall sit and rule on His throne; So He shall be a priest on His throne." Jesus Christ is our heavenly high priest after the order of Melchizedek, a priest-king of old. In the New Testament we learn that Jesus is the Messiah who sits on His throne as both priest and king. Read Hebrews 1:8-9 and Hebrews 6:19-7:28.

Consider Daniel 7:13-14. There it is prophesied that the "Son of Man" comes to the "Ancient of Days" to be "given dominion and glory and a kingdom, that all peoples, nations, and languages should serve Him… which shall not be destroyed." Daniel's vision was NOT that the Son of Man descends to earth to establish His kingdom, but that He ascends to the Ancient of Days—He goes up to heaven to receive His kingdom. In the New Testament we learn that Jesus did ascend to heaven to begin His reign, and that He is reigning now as king of a great people made up of all the tribes of the earth. Read Acts 2:30-39 and 1 Corinthians 15:24-26.

2. Subjects

Understanding that "kingdom" is about exercised rule, who are the people that King Jesus rules? Who are His subjects? This is the next important parallel in seeing Christ's spiritual kingdom.

Are Jesus' subjects all tied to Him by earthly race? Does saying that He is "King of the Jews"—being the deliverer prophesied and promised to the Jews—necessarily exclude the Gentiles? Could the prophesied "King of the Jews" be king over Gentiles as well? According to the Scriptures He can and would. The gospel was for the Jew first, but also for the Greek. Gentiles could partake in the kingdom and its blessings as subjects of King Jesus.

Consider Isaiah 2:2-4. There it is prophesied that "all nations shall flow to" the mountain of the Lord's house. "Many people shall come," and the Lord "shall judge between the nations, and rebuke many people." In the New Testament we learn (initially through Peter, but then also through Paul) that Gentiles were included in the kingdom of Christ. "But God has shown me that I should not call any man common or unclean" (Acts

10:28). Jew and Gentile alike were commanded to be baptized in the name of the Lord for their conversion (Acts 2:38; 10:48) and would be saved in like manner (Acts 15:9, 11). Read Acts 10:34-35.

Members from all nations are subjects of King Jesus, not just Jews. The gospel was to be preached to "every creature" (Mark 16:15). The apostles were commissioned to make disciples from all nations (Matthew 28:19-20). The subjects of King Jesus are "whosoever will" become His subjects by faithful obedience. Read Romans 10:12-13 and Revelation 22:17.

3. Law

How shall King Jesus rule His subjects in His spiritual kingdom? Is He capricious? Is He a despot? In fact, it is Jesus Christ who will execute final judgment on every soul (John 5:22-23; Acts 10:42; 17:31). King Jesus determines who enters heaven and who goes to hell (2 Corinthians 5:10).

Consider Isaiah 2:3. There it is prophesied, "out of Zion shall go forth the law, and the word of the Lord from Jerusalem." The word of God is the law of Christ's kingdom. The terms of pardon and admission to His church were first declared on the Day of Pentecost in Jerusalem (Acts 2:36-47). The law went forth from there. The apostles' doctrine is the word of God that governs all people forever after (Acts 2:42; 1 Thessalonians 2:13). The apostles were chosen ambassadors, inspired by the Holy Spirit, and spoke with the authority of King Jesus. Read 2 Thessalonians 2:15; 3:4, 6, 14 and 2 Peter 3:1-2 and 1 Corinthians 14:37. Thus the New Testament is the law of Christ's kingdom.

It is a perfect law (James 1:25; 2:12). In it Christians find liberty from their sin and all the base powers that bring sinners into condemnation. Christ's law is sufficient to govern His people. Read 2 Timothy 3:16-17 and 2 Peter 1:3. There is no place for His law to be amended by human tradition, the creeds of men, or even the words of angels (Matthew 15:8-9; Galatians 1:6-9; Jude 3).

Jesus Christ is a just king who will judge everyone according to His law, the word of God, NOT according to capricious whims. Read John 12:48. He is governing His subjects by His word today.

4. Territory

The final parallel between earthly kingdoms and Christ's spiritual kingdom for us to consider is territory. As has been established, there is a sense in which Christ's territory or realm is in no way physical. It is not tied to Jerusalem or any part of Palestine (John 4:19-24). The kingdom of God is the exercised sovereignty of God in the hearts of men (Luke 17:20-21).

But there is another sense in which it must be recognized that the territory of the Messiah's kingdom encompasses the entire world.

Consider Daniel 2:34-35, 44. God chose to show king Nebuchadnezzar "what will come to pass after this" (Daniel 2:45). And in his dream he saw "the stone that struck the image became a great mountain and filled the whole earth." The stone was the kingdom of God that would be established in the days of the Roman Empire. It would start small but then increase and expand into the whole earth. Jesus said as much of His kingdom. Read Matthew 13:31-32.

Consider Isaiah 2:2-4. All the nations will come into the house of God. The fact that members of every nation will become members of God's house shows us there is no earthly limit to the territory of Christ's kingdom. Wherever the word is preached to receptive hearts, the kingdom will soon be there. It is for all nations. Read Romans 16:25-26.

Do not forget that the apostles were sent into all the world, to preach the gospel and make disciples of all nations (Matthew 28:18-20; Mark 16:15-16). So the territory of Christ's kingdom is "all the world," because people from every tribe and every nation will believe and obey the gospel to be translated into His kingdom of the redeemed (Colossians 1:13-14).

There is abundant scriptural evidence to show that Jesus Christ possesses a kingdom today. But His spiritual kingdom does not look like the kingdoms of the world in many respects. The lion leads a pride of lambs. As citizens of Jesus' kingdom, Christians had better recognize the differences.

The Kingdom That Doesn't Look Like a Kingdom

Consider a few key distinctions between the spiritual kingdom of Jesus Christ and the kingdoms of the world.

Christ's kingdom has a different idea of greatness than the kingdoms of the world. Mark 10:35-45 shows that greatness is understood in earthly kingdoms to mean *lording* one's will over another. Power is the mark of success, and the more accolades a man can achieve, the greater his status and position. But this is not so in Jesus' kingdom. The greatest of His citizens is the servant of all! Humility is the value that is prized above all others. This is demonstrated by the example of the king who washed His servants' feet (John 13:3-17). Indeed, Jesus was "slave of all" and gave His life a ransom for many.

Christ's kingdom has a different idea of riches than the kingdoms of the world. Moses is held up as an example before kingdom citizens as one who prized Christ greater than earthly riches (Hebrews 11:24-26). The treasures of Egypt and passing pleasures of sin (decadence that is afforded to those of great wealth and ease) meant nothing to him. In fact, Matthew 6:19-21 shows that obsession with material wealth is futile. People are afflicted with many sorrows when greed rules their hearts (1 Timothy 6:9-10). And so kingdom citizens seek to give earthly wealth to those in need, and their ambition is for greater spiritual treasure and blessing in Christ. However, earthly kingdoms see riches as accumulating material wealth. They are far more interested in economic outcomes than the spiritual state of affairs. Jesus' subjects know that if they seek the spiritual first, God will provide for their physical needs (Matthew 6:33). Yet the world places physical needs as paramount and often will let the spiritual take care of itself.

Christ's kingdom has a different idea about life than the kingdoms of the world. Jesus' subjects are to be sacrificial for Him and His cause. Only by living as sacrifices will they gain life everlasting (Mark 8:34-38; Romans 12:1-2). You have to lose your life to save it. This is contrary to the way of the world. Worldly kingdoms only see that life is kept by saving it at all costs—even by taking the life of others. Christians realize that a far greater existence is in store for them beyond this world. There is an eternal life that is in view.

Christ's kingdom has a different idea about love than the kingdoms of the world. Jesus commanded the love of His people to extend beyond blood-ties or marriage. Christians love their God, their brethren, their neighbors…and their enemies (Matthew 5:43-48; 22:37-40; 1 Peter 2:17). But worldly kingdoms only love their selves and their friends or allies. Foreign to the kingdoms of the world is the *Agape* of the Bible.

Christ's kingdom has a different idea about militancy than the kingdoms of the world. Jesus told Pilate that one of the proofs of the other-worldly nature of His kingdom was that His servants did not rise up to deliver Him (John 18:36). Christ's followers are never to use carnal weapons as tools to expand the borders of His kingdom (Matthew 26:52). Obviously, kingdoms of the world go to war in order to grow and subdue other kingdoms. This is not to say that Christ's kingdom is at peace. In fact, there is warfare to be conducted—but it is spiritual. Christ's subjects are to put on the full armor of God in order to battle error and evil, and so rescue souls by the gospel of Jesus Christ (Ephesians 6:10-18; 2 Corinthians 10:3-6). Christ does not ask His servants to take life; they are to give up all, including their own life, to be faithful to Him (Revelation 2:10).

Here are but five distinctions between Christ's kingdom and the kingdoms of the earth. But even these five are enough to show that Christ's kingdom does not look like worldly kingdoms. However, it is the great kingdom of prophecy. It is the glorious spiritual body for which the Old Testament prophets yearned and the New Testament apostles proclaimed! It does not look like the carnal kingdom that dispensationalists and other millennialists are preaching, but it is the glorious kingdom that the Bible reveals.

And why would this surprise anyone? Jesus did not look like the warrior-king that the Jews expected, but He was in actuality their warrior-king—spiritually. Likewise the kingdom of Christ does not look like the triumphant body of world domination that the Jews expected, but it is in actuality the everlasting kingdom that has grown to fill the whole earth—spiritually!

Lesson 11 Questions

1. What is the primary meaning for "kingdom" in the Bible?

2. What is the secondary meaning for "kingdom"?

3. What four things constitute a kingdom?

4. What did Jeremiah 23:5-6 prophesy concerning the Messianic king?

5. What did Isaiah 9:6-7 prophesy concerning the Messianic king?

6. What did Daniel 7:13-14 say about the Messianic king?

7. Who are King Jesus' subjects?

8. What scriptures teach that Christ's kingdom includes both Jew and Gentile?

9. Who executes the final judgment of all mankind?

10. What is the law of Christ's kingdom?

11. Who did Jesus appoint to authoritatively set forth His law, His word?

12. What is the territory of Christ's kingdom?

13. What New Testament teaching coincides with the Daniel 2:35 vision of the Messianic kingdom?

14. Explain "greatness" in Christ's kingdom.

15. Explain "riches" in Christ's kingdom.

16. Explain "militancy" in Christ's kingdom.

Part III

His Promised Return

The Second Coming of Christ

Christ rules His kingdom today. The Messianic kingdom of prophecy arrived right on time in connection with the appearance of Jesus Christ and His fulfilled work. However, the majority of self-professed Christians in today's religious landscape deny that Jesus is reigning in act and in fact. They prefer the idea of a "king in absentia." And they say the kingdom has, at best, partially come. Of course, dispensationalists would even deny the partial establishment of Christ's kingdom, since God can only begin His Old Testament prophetic timetable once the church is "raptured" from the earth. Recall, they hold that God has two peoples: earthly Israel and the spiritual church. But He only deals with them one at a time.

Postmillennialism, historic premillennialism, and dispensationalism all hold that the kingdom is yet future and will be physical. And most teach that the establishment of the kingdom is tied, in some way, to the second coming of Christ. The third and final section of this study pertains to His promised return.

The second coming of Christ is a subject that has spawned much speculation and false teaching. The systems that deny Christ's kingdom came upon His first advent (Mark 1:14-15), in the first century (Mark 9:1), hang all their hopes for a kingdom on the second coming. Very elaborate schemes and charts have been developed to demonstrate all the signs and scenarios that the Bible supposedly teaches will precede the second coming. In this lesson, certain teachings connected to Jesus' second coming will be presented and examined in light of the Scriptures. Christians eagerly anticipate the moment of the Lord's return. This is not because they will finally get a kingdom on earth, but because His kingdom will be free of the earth to be with Him in heaven forever.

There Will Be a Second Coming

Jesus comforted His apostles with the promise that He would "come again" (John 14:1-3). Many of Christ's parables implicitly promise His return. There is an emphasis placed upon the Lord's return and judgment upon His people. In the parable of the wheat and tares, He will return and distinguish the good from the evil (Matthew 13:40-43). In the parable of the wise and foolish virgins, Christ taught His followers to live in constant preparedness for a coming and judgment that they do not expect (Matthew 25:1-13). Again, in the parable of the talents, the Lord returns for a reckoning with His servants. He expects them to be active and diligently working until His return (Matthew 25:14-30).

The angels said that Christ would return (Acts 1:9-11). And the apostles preached and prayed that Christ would come.

- Paul instructed the Christians at Corinth that the Lord's Supper would continue in the assemblies of the church until Jesus comes (1 Corinthians 11:26). He prayed, "O Lord, come!" (1 Corinthians 16:22).
- Peter wrote, "The day of the Lord will come as a thief in the night…" (2 Peter 3:10).
- John prayed, "Even so, come, Lord Jesus!" (Revelation 22:20).
- Early Christians were taught to wait for the second coming, when the wicked would be punished, and the righteous would be vindicated (1 Thessalonians 1:9-10; 2 Thessalonians 1:6-10).

All of these passages show that there will be a second coming. What a blessing to be a Christian living at the moment of Christ's return. How glorious to be found vigilant, diligent, loving, and faithful when Jesus comes. How terrible and horrific to be wicked, worldly, or a wayward Christian when He comes.

Are We in the Last Days?

Understanding the promise that Jesus will come again, are we living in the final days prior to His return? Many popular books, like

Hal Lindsey's *The Late Great Planet Earth,* and Edgar Whisenant's *On Borrowed Time: 88 Reasons Why the Rapture Could Come in 1988*, tied "the last days" and the "last generation" to the generation living when Israelites would come back to Palestine. Within a generation (defined as 40 years) of Israel's "restoration," Jesus would come. At the time of this writing, it is 2008, and there is still no Rapture. Jesus has not come again (See Appendix).

The Bible speaks of the "last days," but it has nothing to do with a State of Israel in Palestine. The New Testament says that we are living in the "last days" (Hebrews 1:1-2; James 5:1-3; 1 Peter 1:20-21). Christians are living in the "last days," and we have been for approximately 2000 years. The phrase "the last days" in Scripture means the last dispensation or era of time.

"God, who at various times and in various ways spoke in time past to the fathers by the prophets, has in these last days spoken to us by His Son, whom He has appointed heir of all things, through whom also He made the worlds," (Hebrews 1:1-2).

The Hebrew writer explains that God has not always communicated with people in the same way. He has revealed His word and meted out blessings and punishments in different ways at different times. There are three clear eras or dispensations of time:

- The Patriarchal Dispensation – God spoke to the fathers of families directly.
- The Mosaic Dispensation – God spoke through Moses, scripture, and prophets to national Israel.
- The Christian Dispensation – God speaks through Jesus, Lord and Christ, and His gospel to the world.

The "last days" were prophesied in the Old Testament (Isaiah 2:2). A sign of their arrival was mentioned in Joel 2:28-29. When Peter preached on Pentecost, He said that "the last days" had arrived (Acts 2:16-21). Similarly, John wrote that it was the "last hour" (1 John 2:18). And Paul warned Timothy about perilous times that would arise in the "last days."

He told Timothy to "turn away" from such people. This means that Paul wasn't telling Timothy about things he would never encounter—things pertaining to some far-future "last days." Paul wasn't confusing Timothy by issuing instructions that were exclusively meant for people 2,000 years later! Timothy, too, was in the "last days."

The New Testament does not prophesy another dispensation. Christians are not awaiting another dispensation—this is the last one. These are "the last days." And that means that Christ will come at the end of this dispensation. But only God determines when a dispensation ends. He could come tomorrow. He could tarry another 2,000 years or more. It's up to Him. And we are told that He is longsuffering and allows time to continue so that more people might be saved in Christ (2 Peter 3:9, 15). We are also told that Jesus will come when people least expect it (Matthew 24:44).

Are There Signs of His Return?

Jesus will come again. The "last days" ends with the final day—the Day of the Lord (2 Peter 3:7, 10). Does the New Testament give signs that will precede the last day and Christ's return?

Dispensationalists like Mark Hitchchock believe that it does. He wrote, "In His great prophetic sermon in Mathew 24-25, Jesus gave the basic outline of the events that will immediately precede His coming. It's Jesus' forecast of the future. And there's no place in the Bible that gives a clearer, more concise overview of what's going to happen during earth's final days."[65]

Matthew 24-25 certainly forecasted future events in store for His Mt. Olivet audience, but all of the "signs" He mentioned pertained solely to the destruction of Herod's temple and Jerusalem, which He had prophesied earlier (Matthew 24:1-2). Jesus' teachings must be kept in the context of the questions that the disciples' asked (Matthew 24:3). And they wanted to know a couple of things:

1) WHEN will the Temple stones be thrown down?
2) WHAT will be the SIGN of your coming, and of the end of the age?

Johnny Stringer suggested that in the mind of the disciples these two events were connected. He wrote:

> A consideration of the accounts of Mark and Luke (Mark 13:4; Luke 21:7) along with that of Matthew confirms our point… the disciples thought the destruction of Jerusalem would come at the end of the world. According to all three accounts, the disciples asked when "those things" (the temples' destruction) would be. But notice the question about the sign: Matthew says they asked for the sign of his coming and the end of the world, but Mark and Luke say they asked for the sign of "these things" (things involved in the destruction of the temple). *In the minds of the disciples, to ask for the sign of the end of the world was the same as to ask for the sign of the temple's destruction.*[66]

If that was the case, then Jesus' words would have clarified for them that the Temple's destruction was not related to the second coming of Christ. There were several signs of the impending destruction of Jerusalem that, if heeded, would save the lives of Christians who escaped the city's terrible fate (Matthew 24:4-22, 32-33). It would occur before that generation passed away (Matthew 24:34). In fact, it occurred in 70 A.D.

Jesus then goes on to say that "Heaven and earth will pass away" (Matthew 24:35). And in connection with this event, also termed "the coming of the Son of Man" (Matthew 24:37, 39, 44), and the coming of the Lord (Matthew 24:42), there are no signs that precede it (Matthew 24:36-44). So Jesus warns His disciples to be faithful and busy, never doubting His return. He teaches them using a story about two servants and an absent master (Matthew 24:45-51).

To be sure, there is challenging language in Matthew 24. Particularly as Mathew 24:29-31 are read, people may question how that could pertain to the destruction of Jerusalem. In what way did that come to pass within the generation (Matthew 24:34)? Matthew 24:29-31 should be understood as an elaboration upon the "tribulation" mentioned in verse 21. Jesus is speaking as a prophet, declaring God's judgment upon a nation: God's judgment is coming upon Jerusalem. As such, Jesus adopts the language of previous prophets of God who proclaimed judgment upon nations. It is symbolic and potent. As Currie wrote, "Apocalyptic literature uses dramatic imagery of cataclysmic disruptions to describe changes within the human political sphere."[67]

Consider Matthew 24:29. Jesus says, "the sun will be darkened, and the moon will not give its light; the stars will fall from heaven, and the powers of the heavens will be shaken." Jesus is not talking about the end of the cosmos here. If He were, it wouldn't do any good to tell people to escape to the mountains for safety (Matthew 24:16). Jesus is employing the kind of language that the prophet Isaiah used as he pronounced God's judgment on Babylon (Isaiah 13:9-13). God used the Medes to overthrow Babylon—but the literal stars remained in the sky (Isaiah 13:17-19). Isaiah wrote similarly of God's judgment upon Edom (Isaiah 34:4-10). The "host of heaven" did not literally fall to earth, but the powers of Edom were done. The prophet Ezekiel followed the same pattern. He prophesied against Egypt and its Pharaoh (Ezekiel 32:7-8). Egypt would fall, and this is said through the imagery of darkened stars, a covered sun, and the moon not giving light. But we know the sun still shines. Jesus is using prophetic language, prophesying God's judgment on Jerusalem. God would use the Romans to conquer Jerusalem.

Consider Matthew 24:30. Jesus says, "They will see the Son of Man coming on the clouds of heaven with power and great glory." Again, this is prophet's language for God's judgment on nations. "Clouds" and "the day of the Lord" mean God's judgment on a people, but not necessarily the end of the world. Isaiah 19:1 says, "See, the Lord rides on a swift cloud and is coming to Egypt. The idols of Egypt tremble before Him, and the hearts of the Egyptians melt within them." Ezekiel also prophesied against Egypt and wrote that the day of the Lord was a day of clouds (Ezekiel 30:3-4). As Joel warned of the coming Babylonian invasion against Jerusalem, it is called "the day of the Lord… a day of darkness and gloominess, a day of clouds and thick darkness" (Joel 2:1-2). Jesus' words follow a long line of such prophetic utterance. And we see that these things were fulfilled within that generation at the destruction of Jerusalem (Matthew 24:34).

Consider Matthew 24:31. Jesus continues with, "He will send His angels with a great sound of a trumpet, and they will gather together His elect from the four winds, from one end of heaven to the other." Christ follows the prophetic pattern again. Through the trumpet symbol, Isaiah declared that captive Jews of Assyria and Egypt should be called to Jerusalem. Isaiah 27:13, "So it shall be in that day: The great trumpet will be blown; They will come, who are about to perish in the land of Assyria, And they who are outcasts in the land of Egypt, And shall worship the LORD in the holy mount at Jerusalem." There was not a gigantic trumpet. But it meant a calling. Jesus shows how His people, His elect, are called out from all over the world—"the four winds, from one end of heaven to another." The Temple, Jerusalem, and the Jewish system will be no more, but that does not mean Jesus Christ does not have a people. It means His people are spiritual, made of up all races—not earthly, tied to one race. This word was certainly fulfilled as His messengers carried the gospel all over the world.

There will be no signs of Jesus' second coming. It will be like a thief in the night (2 Peter 3:10; 1 Thessalonians 5:1-2). Therefore, Christians must be prepared for His return at all times (1 Thessalonians 5:3-10; Matthew 24:45-25:13).

Will There Be a Rapture?

In attempting to chart dispensationalism, it is evident that the teaching holds to several "second" comings. It is the fact of their teaching, though they usually deny it. They say they believe in one second coming, but that it has two parts: the Rapture and the Revelation.

The word Rapture is used to describe a secret snatching away of the church, both the dead and living saints, who are caught up to meet the Lord in the air. Sometimes the term "translation" of the saints is used as well. The Rapture is a silent and unwarned disappearance of all the Christians. They vanish—they're just gone and, of course, most people are "left behind." The Revelation is when Jesus comes back to earth with those raptured saints to establish the earthly kingdom.

The error of the Rapture doctrine is easily seen by any who would care to make a fair investigation on the subject. Does the Bible teach it? The first challenge is the concordance, because when you look up "Rapture" in there, you will not find it. The word does not appear in the Bible. So you can't just "look it up"—you have to do a little digging.

Just because a particular word does not appear in the Scripture does not mean that the idea is foreign to Scripture. But, as we shall see, there is no Bible basis for the doctrine of the Rapture. Even the staunchest proponents of dispensationalism's Rapture have, in moments of unguarded academic honesty, admitted that the Bible does not expressly teach it. As Currie showed:

> For many years, Dr. John Walvoord was president of Dallas Theological Seminary, an institution that has become synonymous with an unwavering allegiance to the rapturist system....
>
> In the first edition of his 1957 book, *The Rapture Question*, Walvoord wrote, "The rapture question is determined more by ecclesiology [theology of the Church] than eschatology [theology of future events, specifically last things]. *Neither posttribulationalism nor pretribulationalism is an explicit teaching of Scripture. The Bible does not in so many words state it*" (*TRQ*, forward; emphasis added)....
>
> The admission—that the believer's rapture is not a clear and concise teaching of the Bible—was so explosive that in all future editions of this book it was deleted. Lack of clear biblical support is the elephant in the living room that all educated rapturists know exists, but never discuss. But there it is: nowhere does one passage of the Bible speak of both the rapture and the second coming. Nowhere does one passage of the Bible lay out the time scheme that rapturists must justify by piecing one verse here with another verse there.[68]

Rapturists first seek to prove their theory by emphasizing two Greek words and suggesting that the use of these two words means two exclusive events. The first word, PAROUSIA, means "coming," and appears in 1 Thessalonians 4:15. They say this is the secret coming of Jesus to quietly whisk away the Christians and leave many behind. The second word is EPIPHANIA, which means "appearance." We find this word in 1 Timothy 6:14. They say this is the glorious appearance of Christ with His saints at the end of the seven-year Great Tribulation to establish His kingdom. This distinction of terms is artificial. As 2 Thessalonians 2:8 demonstrates, both words are used to speak of the same occasion. "And then the lawless one will be revealed, whom the Lord will consume with the breath of His mouth and destroy with the brightness [EPIPHANIA] of His coming [PAROUSIA]," (2 Thessalonians 2:8).

Rapturists turn to 1 Thessalonians 4:14-18 as the proof-text for their doctrine. Proponents believe that the Rapture can be taught and defended from this passage. Read these verses and consider whether they actually say what is needed to support the Rapture theory.

- It is observed that the word "Rapture" is absent from these verses as well as the rest of the Bible.
- The verses do not teach a secret or silent resurrection (verse 16); instead, it says that there will be a "shout," "voice of an archangel," and "the trumpet of God."
- The verses do not hint at a return to earth of the saints who have been caught up to Christ (verse 17). Evidently, they fly up to be with Jesus in the air, and they stay with Jesus forever. This verse does not say that Jesus will touch terra firma. There is no New Testament scripture that teaches Jesus will put His feet back on the ground.
- The verses are written for Christians to encourage and give hope to those who are mourning the passing of their Christian loved ones—those asleep in Jesus (verses 13-14, 18). The resurrection of the wicked is not contemplated in the context at all. There is no reason to believe that there are multiple resurrections, especially since Christ speaks of one general resurrection (John 5:28-29).

The other common Rapture text is back in Matthew 24. Read Matthew 24:36-42. At first glance it may sound like the Rapture to hear of one person in the field being taken and another is left. But what is Jesus saying in this paragraph? He is explaining the suddenness and the lack of signs or warning for His second coming—when the heavens and earth pass away (Matthew 24:35). He is saying how life will continue, as is, until the very moment of His return. People will be eating and drinking. People will be having weddings, people will be in the field farming (that means seasons continue), and people will be about their meals—milling for bread. And without warning, some are "taken." So those who take Jesus as their Lord must ever live with His return in view.

But these verses do not say anything about people being "left behind" for seven years wondering what happened to those around them. Rather these verses in Matthew 24 harmonize perfectly with 1 Thessalonians 4:17-5:4. The Lord comes as a thief in the night. There is no warning. Yet Christians shall not be caught unprepared because they are living ever vigilant for His return. Those Christians who are living at the Day of the Lord shall fly up to the sky. Those wicked on the earth will have sudden destruction come upon them from which there is no escape. The earth itself is being destroyed by fire (2 Peter 3:7, 10-12).

Mathew 24 does not teach the Rapture. It does not speak of a secret coming nor of a return of Christ or Christians to earth. It does not teach a two-part second coming. It declares one coming of the Son of Man and tells all humanity to be ready for it!

The Rapture is a core tenant of the dispensational system. It allows God to have two peoples. It motivates evangelistic efforts among Rapturists. It fuels political lobbying to make sure nations align in the way necessary to bring it forth. And, of course, it has to happen before Jesus can establish His corporeal kingdom and reign for 1,000 years. But the Scriptures just do not say what they need to in order to establish and sustain this End Times invention of John Nelson Darby. **There is no Rapture.**

When Jesus Comes...

While much of this lesson has been directed at exposing error that is popularly accepted concerning the second coming, let us not forget what the Bible has revealed about the return of the Lord.

Resurrection. When Jesus comes He will raise the dead (John 5:28-29; 1 Thessalonians 4:16). Death shall be overcome with the victory of resurrection. All will be fitted with bodies suitable for eternal existence (1 Corinthians 15:35-49). And none shall ever die again.

Destruction of the Earth. When Jesus comes He will destroy the earth (2 Peter 3:7, 10-12). He is not coming back to live on the earth or reign on the earth, for He is going to burn it up!

Judgment. When Jesus comes He will judge the world (Acts 17:30-31; John 12:48; 2 Corinthians 5:10). The Father has appointed Him to this work.

Heaven, Hell, and Eternity. When Jesus comes He will reward the righteous with the joy of heaven, and He will punish the wicked with the horror of hell (Matthew 25:34, 41, 46).

There is a second coming! Jesus has promised to return! Are you ready?

Lesson 12 Questions

1. Who taught that Jesus would come again?

2. Name one of Jesus' parables that imply a second coming of Christ.

3. What is "the last days" as it is used in the Bible?

4. What is a dispensation?

5. How many dispensations does the Bible reveal? What are their features?

6. What Bible passage is commonly used by dispensationalists to teach that there are signs that will precede the second coming of Christ?

7. List some of the signs that the disciples were told to watch for in Matthew 24:4-21.

8. What did these signs actually precede?

9. What kind of language was Jesus using in Matthew 24:29-31?

10. What does Matthew 24:34 say that tells us Matthew 24:29-31 must have already occurred?

11. Are there signs that precede the second coming of Christ?

12. How is Jesus' second coming described in Matthew 24:35-51?

13. What is the Rapture doctrine that dispensationalists teach?

14. What two words do Rapturists attempt to build their doctrine around? Why doesn't it work?

15. How does 1 Thessalonians 4:13-18 actually disprove the Rapture?

16. Why does dispensationalism fall apart if there is no Rapture?

17. What is Jesus coming back to do?

18. What should Christians take to heart about Christ's promise of the second coming?

Heaven: The Kingdom's Great Reward

Jesus' church is His kingdom. The Messianic kingdom of Old Testament prophecy is the New Testament church of Christ. They are one and the same body of redeemed people. As Marshall Patton observed:

> A further study of the interchangeable use made of the terms "kingdom" and "church" (Matt. 16:18-20; Col. 1:13, 18; Heb. 12:23, 28) shows this kingdom to be the church which was established on the first Pentecost after the resurrection of Christ, a record of which we find in Acts 2. This is corroborated by Paul's statement to the effect that the church is not an accident, afterthought, or substitution, but rather "according to the eternal purpose" of God (Eph. 3:10, 11). It is the same thing God had in mind from eternity, whether it be called "kingdom," "church," or some other divine appellation.[69]

So Christ's kingdom and Christ's church are the same thing. That kingdom which was foretold in the Old Testament is realized in the New Testament church. People become citizens of His kingdom in this life, not some future millennium. When a penitent believer is "baptized into Christ" (Galatians 3:27), he or she is added to His church (Acts 2:38-41, 47). At the same time and in the same way, they are "conveyed" into the kingdom of the Son (Colossians 1:13-14). A member of the church of Christ is a citizen of the kingdom of Christ. And membership matters! Citizenship is essential!

To help see the great importance of being a church member or kingdom subject, just consider another "divine appellation" for God's people: the body.

- Jesus is the head of the body (Ephesians 1:22-23). He is the king of the kingdom, the head of the church.

- Jesus reconciles all people (Jews and Gentiles) to God in the body (Ephesians 2:16; 3:6). All people can be citizens of the kingdom. It is a spiritual kingdom made up of all nations and tribes of men. All people can be members of His church. All people can become His people through the gospel of Christ when they are part of Christ's body!

- There is one body (Ephesians 4:4). There is one people of God. There is one church. There is one kingdom. You are either in His church/kingdom/body, or you are out. And if you are out, then you are not one of His people.

- The body is built up as each member supplies its part (Ephesians 4:11-16). The kingdom is a place for service, accountability, and growth. The church is not hollow ritual, but a vibrant spiritual nation as members develop one another in Christ by His truth! Christ has a role for you in His kingdom, a place for you in His church (Ephesians 5:30).

- Jesus is the savior of the body (Ephesians 5:23). Church membership—kingdom citizenship—is a "salvation issue." In modern denominational vernacular, some disagreements between believers are peripheral issues and some are "salvation issues." They subscribe to the notion of a gospel-doctrine distinction that allows the uneasy union of denominationalism to exist. As long as a denomination subscribes to "core" tenants of Christianity (like the death, burial, and resurrection of Jesus) labeled "gospel" and "salvation issues," then the churches can chart their own course on "secondary" doctrinal issues (for instance, the method or meaning of baptism). Church membership tends to fall in the "secondary" realm because denominations respect all other denominations as valid. The Bible is not so broad. Only one church, one body is revealed (Ephesians 4:4). If a person is not in Christ's body, then He is not their savior.

- Christians are members of His body (Ephesians 5:30). It is amazing that some professed Christians think that church membership is unimportant but being a part of His kingdom is important. Any denomination or group is as good as any other, they say, because ultimately we will all be united in one kingdom on earth. This is a dangerous error. There is only one church, one kingdom. Perish the thought that a person can be right with Jesus while being estranged from His church! If you're not a part of His church, then you are missing His kingdom!

The absolute importance of church membership and kingdom citizenship is clear! Those who desire to go to heaven must be citizens of Christ's kingdom, for theirs is a heavenly citizenship. Let's consider heaven, His kingdom's great reward.

Heaven's Citizens

According to Philippians 3:20-21, Christian "citizenship is in heaven." The Lord Jesus Christ is currently there. His subjects are eagerly waiting for Him to come from there to save them and transform them into a "glorious" body—one fit for eternal existence. Paul wrote of "the working by which He is able even to subdue all things to Himself." When this is compared to 1 Corinthians 15:24-26, it is evident that the last thing to be subdued—"the last enemy that will be destroyed"—is death. Jesus Christ shall destroy death by "working" the resurrection upon His second coming. The power of transformation that will fit His citizens with glorious bodies is resurrection power (1 Corinthians 15:39-55)!

In fact, the Bible teaches a general resurrection (John 5:28-29). When the Lord comes, all will rise from the grave and be fitted with an eternal body. Yet some shall only be raised for torment. Theirs is a "resurrection to condemnation." Jesus Christ will send those who have died in their sins to hell (Mark 9:43-48; Matthew 25:41, 46). But those of His faithful subjects living upon His return shall simply rise to meet Him in the air and be changed into their heavenly form in the twinkling of an eye, without experiencing death (1 Thessalonians 4:17; 1 Corinthians 15:51-53). Though heaven is invisible to us now, one day we will see it (2 Corinthians 4:16-18). God has a body for us that is not physical—"not made with hands"—in heaven. Once we die and shed this earthly "tent," then God can clothe us in the glorious tent (2 Corinthians 5:1-4). One day we shall see Jesus as He is in glory, for we shall be like Him (1 John 3:2). Our physical bodies lack the ability to witness the full glory of God without it killing us (Exodus 33:18-23). But the resurrection body can inherit and enjoy heaven—the eternal abode of God.

King Jesus knows who His people are. The greatest joy that a person can have is the knowledge that their name is written in heaven, as Luke 10:17-20 shows. On that occasion, seventy of the Lord's disciples returned after exercising supernatural power and preaching to communities throughout the region that the Lord was about to travel there (Luke 10:1-16). The disciples returned to Jesus excited about the power that they had exercised by Christ's authority. But Jesus explained, "do not rejoice in this, that the spirits are subject to you, but rather rejoice because your names are written in heaven."

This shows that Christians today—who lack the miraculous spiritual gifts that some first century Christians possessed—still have the same great joy. Our hope, inheritance, and joy are in no way diminished because we live at a later time than they, for all Christians have their names recorded in heaven. Their names are written in the Book of Life along with all of Paul's fellow workers (Philippians 4:3; Revelation 20:12, 15). Their names are registered in heaven along with all of the church of the firstborn (Hebrews 12:23).

Heaven is the great salvation of kingdom citizens (1 Peter 1:3-5). When we became Christians, we were born again to a living hope for an incorruptible inheritance that is reserved in heaven for us. Faith is the power that God keeps us by until the Lord shall return for our salvation. Citizens are saved from the destroyed earth. They are saved from the torment of hell. They are saved for the great reward in heaven (Matthew 5:12).

The promise of heaven shapes the way kingdom citizens think and live today.

Because of Heaven...

Our mind is above (Colossians 3:1-2). Some have criticized Christians in the past saying, "they are so heavenly minded that they are of no earthly good." In fact, a proper focus on our king should make us the most earthly good. What reminds us to be salt and light in this dark and decaying world? It is a focus on our king that reminds us to live righteously, and to zealously do the good works that please Him and bring our fellow man to glorify Him (Matthew 5:13-16). Christians are of the greatest earthly good when they are mindful of the word and will of their king. We need to think about heaven more. We need to think about the Lord and Savior that abides there more! It will help us to keep our priorities straight and to remember what is truly valuable.

Our hope is above (Colossians 1:3-5). Paul wrote the Ephesians that there is one hope (Ephesians 4:4). And to the Colossians he wrote that their hope is laid up in heaven. The gospel is the message that brings the hope of heaven to the world. This hope is not about getting to be carnal rulers on a revamped, utopian earth. In 2 Peter 3:13, we are told to look for new heavens and a new earth. This is an expression that speaks to the Christian's home in heaven. Peter was not confused. In 1 Peter 1:3-5 he wrote of the Christian's living hope: Heaven. When 2 Peter 3:13 is read in context, we see that he wrote of the same thing, just using a figure of speech. The eventual destruction of this physical universe, the "heavens and the earth," is under consideration throughout the third chapter. As Willis observed, "The phrase 'the heavens and the earth' is the equivalent to what we mean by the 'universe.'"[70]

Peter wrote of the past "heavens and the earth," the present "heavens and the earth," and the future "heavens and the earth."

- God made the heavens and the earth – the antediluvian world (2 Peter 3:5).
- God destroyed it with water (2 Peter 3:6).
- God preserves the current heavens and the earth – the postdiluvian world (2 Peter 3:7).
- God will destroy the current heavens and earth with fire (2 Peter 3:7, 10-12).
- God has promised a new heavens and a new earth where righteousness dwells (2 Peter 3:13).

Unlike the antediluvian and postdiluvian physical universe, the new universe is a place of righteousness. No unrighteousness. Righteousness lives or dwells there. The Bible shows us that the place of untainted righteousness is heaven (Revelation 21:1, 27). The new universe, the "new heavens and new earth," is heaven.

Furthermore, there is no reason to think that the new universe is physical, given the great lengths to which Peter describes the destruction of the physical universe, the current "heavens and earth":

- "Reserved for fire" (2 Peter 3:7).
- "The heavens will pass away with a great noise" (2 Peter 3:10).
- "The elements will melt with fervent heat" (2 Peter 3:10).
- "The earth and the works that are in it will be burned up" (2 Peter 3:10).
- "All these things will be dissolved" (2 Peter 3:11).
- "The heavens will be dissolved, being on fire" (2 Peter 3:12).
- "The elements will melt with fervent heat" (2 Peter 3:12).

And this occurs on "the day of judgment" (2 Peter 3:7), which is "the day of the Lord" (2 Peter 3:10), and "the day of God" (2 Peter 3:12). So our hope is for a new place, a new city, a new country, spiritual—not physical or made with hands—where our resurrected bodies live eternally in the righteous light of God (Hebrews 11:8-10, 13-16; 13:14). Our hope is heaven!

Our treasure is above (Matthew 6:19-21; 19:21). The Lord has told us that our heart follows our treasure. He said, "where your treasure is, there your heart will be also." It follows that if our mind and our hope is above, then our heart is above. Jesus counsels us to store up treasures in heaven. We do that as we learn to value what God values, and so invest our resources in the things of God: those things of redemptive and spiritual worth.

So we have seen that the Lord's church is His kingdom. The promise and hope of the heavenly territory is solely the blessing of kingdom citizens. This alters our thinking and heart for the present world. And it also moves us to action!

Until heaven...

Christians must honor the king. Citizens need to exalt, glorify, and worship their king during their time on earth. In fact, such honor and praise can never be exhausted. Looking to heaven's throne room through John's Book of Revelation, we hear, "Worthy is the Lamb who was slain to receive power and riches and wisdom and strength and honor and glory and blessing" and "Blessing and honor and glory and power be to Him who sits on the throne, and to the Lamb, forever and ever!" (Revelation 5:12-13). And among the heavenly hosts praising Jesus, there is that multitude of redeemed who have been made a kingdom by the blood of the lamb (Revelation 5:9-10). When local churches assemble for worship, the prayers, hymns, and fellowship are a sweet foretaste of heaven. If Christians do not honor the king, who will?

Christians must heed the king. To "heed" is to obey. Kingdom citizens may praise Jesus until they are blue in the face, but it is surely vain if they are not faithful subjects to His rule. Jesus raised a fair question for His disciples in Luke 6:46, "But why do you call Me 'Lord, Lord,' and not do the things which I say?"

King Saul learned this lesson the hard way. When he did not do all that God had commanded him, Samuel instructed that rebellious man saying, "Has the Lord as great delight in burnt offerings and sacrifices, as in obeying the voice of the Lord? Behold, to obey is better than sacrifice, and to heed than the fat of rams" (1 Samuel 15:22). Saul lost his kingdom. Christians stand to lose much more. Citizens can expect fiery judgment in return for their willful sin against their redeemer and king (Hebrews 10:26-31). Until Jesus returns, Christians need to be obedient above all.

Christians must herald the king. Citizens proclaim, preach, and herald their king! It's not just preachers that do all the preaching necessary for the kingdom to grow. Gospel preachers have an important work in faithfully preaching Christ, just as Philip the evangelist did (Acts 8:5). That blessed message concerns "the kingdom of God," "the name of Jesus Christ," and baptism (Acts 8:12). Yet Luke records that all Christians "went everywhere preaching the word" (Acts 8:4), and not just evangelists like

Philip. Citizens of Christ's kingdom need to declare as well as model the faith. We herald the king when we speak the good news as well as live it.

May God bless His kingdom to do these things until King Jesus returns to take them to the reward of heaven! Never lose heart or doubt the Lord. Remember, the lion is the lamb!

Lesson 13 Questions

1. Name some terms the Bible uses to describe the group of people redeemed in Christ. Give a scripture where that term is used.

2. How many bodies of redeemed people are there?

3. Do you think that many people accept that idea that there is only one church? Why or why not?

4. How would you show someone that there is only one church?

5. Is church membership a salvation issue? Why or why not?

6. What does it mean to have a citizenship in heaven?

7. What should Christians rejoice the most about?

8. How do Christians set their minds above?

9. What is the Christian's one hope?

10. What "heavens and the earth" does Peter consider in 2 Peter 3?

11. What will God do to the current heavens and earth?

12. How do Christians store up treasures in heaven?

13. What three things do kingdom citizens need to do until the king comes?

14. What are some of your personal responsibilities as a citizen of Christ's kingdom?

If You Are Reading This, They Were Wrong

The truth is that no one knows or can know when the world will end. Jesus said, "But of that day and hour no one knows, not even the angels of heaven, but My Father only" (Matthew 24:36). Christians are told to be vigilant and diligent, because the Lord's return shall be "like a thief in the night."

This has not stopped numerous self-appointed prophets and "prophecy experts" from setting dates for the end of the world. With no exceptions, the published date for Christ's return has come and gone without His arrival. This error moves the presumptuous teacher from the category of "prophecy expert" to false prophet.

"But the prophet who presumes to speak a word in My name, which I have not commanded him to speak… that prophet shall die…. when a prophet speaks in the name of the LORD, if the thing does not happen or come to pass, that is the thing which the LORD has not spoken; the prophet has spoken it presumptuously; you shall not be afraid of him" (Deuteronomy 18:20-22).

While some "prophecy experts" have been disgraced and ruined over their failed predictions, it's shocking to observe how many manage to maintain influence and a following despite their blatant and rebellious error.

The following list of date-setters is presented to humble every believer. If our zeal for the Lord is not according to knowledge, our best intentions may turn into stumbling blocks. The foolishness of date-setting only gives the world opportunity to mock and discredit the Faith. The world doesn't stop to consider that the date-setters themselves have transgressed God's revelation in their false prophecies—they only see zealous fools calling out for the return of a god that never comes.

May reflection upon this list safeguard us from ever being so presumptuous or foolish or taken with our own End Times speculations that we set a date and join an ominous list of false prophets.

If you are reading this list, then the people on it were wrong! The left column lists the order in which the person (or group) lived and set a date for the end of the world. The right column is the date that was set… and has passed without Christ's return.

The Date-Setter	**Predicted Date of the End**
1. Ignatius	100 AD
2. Montanus, founder Montanism movement	150-179 AD
3. Cyprian	250 AD
4. Irenaeus	1000 AD
5. Hippolytus	500 AD
6. Julius Africanus	500 AD
7. St. Martin of Tours	470 AD
8. Prophetess Thiota	848 AD
9. The Prophet Muhammad, founder Islam	1110 AD
10. Beatus, Abbot of Liebana	796 AD
11. St. Gregory of Tours	799-806 AD
12. Bernard of Thuringa	992 AD
13. Kaiser Otto III	1000 AD
14. Joachim Fiore	1260 AD
15. The Taborites sect	1420 AD
16. Melchoir Hoffmann	1533 AD
17. Jan Matthys	1534 AD
18. Christopher Columbus	1656 AD
19. Deacon William Aspinwall	1673 AD
20. Cotton Mather	1697 AD
21. The Shakers sect	1792 AD
22. Martin Luther	1800s AD

23. John Napier of Merchiston   1688-1700 AD

24. The Fifth Monarchy Men   1650-1700 AD

25. John Mason, rector of Water Stratford in Buckinghamshire 1694 AD

26. Joseph Smith, founder Mormonism   1888 AD

27. William Miller, founder Millerites   1843-1844 AD

28. Rev. M. Baxter (Church of England)   1868 AD

29. Edward Irving   1868 AD

30. Lee T. Spangler   1908 AD

31. Robert Milligan   1922 AD

32. Charles Taze Russell, founder Jehovah's Witnesses 1914 AD

33. "Judge" Joseph F. Rutherford   1925 AD

34. Oswald J. Smith   1933 AD

35. W.E. Blackstone   1934-1935 AD

36. Herbert W. Armstrong, founder Worldwide Church of God 1936 AD

37. Billy Graham   1952 AD

38. Charles Laughhead   1954 AD

39. Charles Taylor   1975 AD

40. Nathan Knorr   1975 AD

41. Hal Lindsey   1988 AD

42. Chuck Smith   1981 AD

43. Pat Robertson   1982 AD

44. Edgar C. Whisenant   1988 -1989 AD

45. David Koresch   1995 AD

46. Harold Camping   1994 AD

47. Jack Van Impe   1996 AD

48. Lester Sumrall   2000 AD

49. Grant Jeffrey   2000 AD

50. Paul Crouch, founder Trinity Broadcasting Network 2005-2010 AD

Amillennialism – The eschatological viewpoint that there will be no corporeal thousand year reign of Christ. The Messianic kingdom (or kingdom of God) is currently present in the world as Christ rules His church. Revelation 20 is symbolic.

Armageddon – Hebrew for "Mount of Megiddo." In the premillennial system this is the great earthly battle where Jesus and His saints conquer evil earthly forces to deliver the State of Israel. It is better understood as a symbol for God's ultimate overthrow of evil (Revelation 16:16).

Christ – According to John 1:41 and John 4:25, this is the Greek translation for Messiah. It means "anointed one." This is the prophesied deliverer and savior for sinful mankind.

Christendom – In this book, this is an umbrella term to speak of all adherents to some kind of Christianity.

Denominationalism – "Diverse religious traditions and organizations that openly compete for adherents while respecting other religious organizations as valid."[71]

Dispensationalism – A kind of premillennialism known for its woodenly literal method of interpretation (particularly of Old Testament prophecy) and its insistence that God has two chosen peoples: earthly Jews and the spiritual church. God has purposes and plans for both groups, and He will uniquely save them both. The cornerstone tenet of Dispensationalism is the Rapture doctrine.

Ecclesiology – The theological study of the doctrine of church.

Eschatology – The theological study of the doctrine of final things or last things.

Hermeneutics – The science of the interpretation of Scripture.

Inspiration – Literally, "God breathed" (2 Timothy 3:16). The doctrine that the Scriptures are entirely the word of God and not the inventions or interpolations of men.

Irgun – A militant Israeli organization that waged guerilla warfare against Palestinian Arabs and British forces from 1931-1948 with the goal of securing "every Jew's right to enter Palestine" regardless of immigration law.

Kingdom – Two meanings: The first or primary meaning is exercised authority, sovereignty, and reign. Secondarily, the word communicates territory or realm in subject.

Messiah – Hebrew word meaning "anointed one." Designated the prophesied deliverer, prophet, and king of Israel. In the New Testament it is translated "Christ" (John 1:41; 4:25).

Millennium – A thousand years. In theological / eschatological studies it pertains to the interpretation of the reign of Jesus Christ in Revelation 20.

Numerology – The study of the relationship of numbers as symbols in literature. Within highly symbolic prophetic scriptures, the numbers signify meanings as well.

Postmillennialism – The eschatological viewpoint that the world gets better and better by the influence and acceptance of the gospel until a thousand year "golden age" of humanity occurs. At the conclusion of the thousand years of gospel triumph, Jesus returns.

Premillennialism – The eschatological viewpoint that the world gets worse and worse, evil increases until Jesus comes, subdues all evil, and establishes His kingdom on earth to rule for a thousand years.

Prophecy Experts – In this book, this is an umbrella term used to describe current popular, widely studied and published, preachers and teachers of dispensationalism. Many authors of dispensational volumes are labeled "prophecy expert" on the book jacket.

Rapture – The cornerstone event of dispensational eschatology. It is the secret snatching away of the church that plunges the world into a seven-year period of Tribulation and wickedness until Jesus finally returns with His saints to wage the battle of Armageddon. This event is the hinge that allows Darby's "two peoples of God" theory to play out. If the Rapture is not biblical, then the whole dispensational system falls.

Theology – The study of God, the things of God, and discernment of biblical doctrine.

Tribulation – Terrible physical trial, hardship, and persecution. Jesus used the term to speak of the destruction of Jerusalem (Matthew 24:1-3, 21). He also spoke of it to His apostles to warn of worldly opposition to their work (John 16:33). Within dispensationalism it refers to a set seven-year period—beginning with the Rapture and ending with Christ's return for Armageddon—where evil forces hunt down and persecute Christians.

Zionism – A nineteenth century sociopolitical movement for the reunion of Jews out of their European dispersion and the establishment of a sovereign Jewish State in the land of Palestine.

1 J. Dwight Pentecost, Things to Come. (Grand Rapids, MI: Zondervan Publishing House, 1964) 1.
2 Stafford North, Unlocking Revelation. (Nashville, TN: 21ˢᵗ Century Christian, 2003) 14.
3 North, 15.
4 John E. Walvoord, The Millennial Kingdom. (Grand Rapids, MI: Zondervan Publishing House, 1959) vii.
5 Don Simpson, Kingdom Prophecy in Review. (Fort Worth, TX: Star Bible Publications, 2002) 1.
6 Charles M. Neal, Light in a Dark Place, 55. Quoted in Neal-Wallace Discussion on The Thousand Years Reign of Christ. (Firm Foundation Publishing House. Reprint, 1933) 324.
7 This list taken from a sermon, "Hand of Deliverance in the Bible" by Z.T. Sweeney.
8 John Hagee, In Defense of Israel. (Lake Mary, FL: FrontLine, 2007) 136.
9 Hagee, 137.
10 Hagee, 136-140.
11 Hagee, 134.
12 Hagee, 135-136.
13 Hagee, 134.
14 Hagee, 140-141, 143.
15 Fausset's Bible Dictionary, Electronic Database Copyright (c)1998 by Biblesoft.
16 T.C. Horton and Charles E. Hurlburt. Names of Christ. (Chicago, IL: Moody Press, 1994) 12.
17 Homer Hailey, Revelation: An Introduction and Commentary. (Louisville, KY: Religious Supply Inc. 1992) 176-177.
18 Foy E Wallace, Jr., God's Prophetic Word. (Oklahoma City, OK. Foy E. Wallace Jr. Publications, 1960) 214.
19 Wallace, 217.
20 MacArthur, John. "Kingdom Parables: Matthew 13:1-2." www.gty.org. downloaded 1/17/06, 3-4.
21 MacArthur, 4.
22 MacArthur, 4.
23 H. Leo Boles, Boles-Boll Debate: A Discussion on Prophetic and Premillennial Themes. (Indianapolis, IN: Faith and Facts Press, Reprint, 1992) 218-219.
24 MacArthur, 6.
25 Don Simpson, Kingdom Prophecy in Review. (Fort Worth, TX: Star Bible Publications, 2002) 36-37.
26 Jim McGuiggan, The Reign of God. (Fort Worth, TX: Star Bible Publications, 1992) 25.
27 Dave Ramsey, The Total Money Makeover. (Nashville, TN: Thomas Nelson Inc., 2003) 50.
28 from The Online Bible Thayer's Greek Lexicon and Brown Driver & Briggs Hebrew Lexicon, Copyright (c)1993, (Woodside Bible Fellowship, Ontario, Canada). Licensed from the Institute for Creation Research.
29 from Vine's Expository Dictionary of Biblical Words, Copyright (c)1985, Thomas Nelson Publishers.
30 from The Online Bible Thayer's Greek Lexicon and Brown Driver & Briggs Hebrew Lexicon, Copyright (c)1993, (Woodside Bible Fellowship, Ontario, Canada). Licensed from the Institute for Creation Research.
31 McGuiggan, 15.
32 George Eldon Ladd. The Gospel of the Kingdom. 19. Quoted in McGuiggan, 113.
33 Theodor Herzl. The Jewish State. Filiquarian Publishing, LLC, 2006. 74.
34 David B. Currie, Rapture: the end-times error that leaves the Bible behind. (Manchester, NH: Sophia Institute Press, 2003) 15.
35 McGuiggan, 17.
36 Rod Rutherford, The Millennial Mania: A Study of Premillennialism. 1.

37 Tim LaHaye's introduction for Hitchcock, Mark and Thomas Ice. The Truth Behind Left Behind. (Sisters, OR: Multnomah Publishers, 2004) 5-6.
38 David B. Currie, Rapture. (Manchester, NH: Sophia Institute Press, 2003) 45.
39 Don Simpson, Kingdom Prophecy in Review. (Fort Worth, TX: Star Bible Publications, 1977) 3.
40 The New International Dictionary of the Christian Church, J.D. Douglas, editor, 794.
41 George Eldon Ladd, The Meaning of the Millennium: Four Views. Editor Robert G. Clouse. (Downers Grove, IL: Intervarsity, 1977) 27.
42 Charles Ryrie, Dispensationalism Today. (Chicago, IL: Moody Press, 1965) 45.
43 Rutherford, 4.
44 Timothy P. Weber, On The Road to Armageddon: how evangelicals became Israel's best friend. (Grand Rapids, MI: Baker Academic, 2004) 21.
45 John F. Walvoord, The Millennial Kingdom. (Grand Rapids, MI: Zondervan, 1959) 5.
46 A Dictionary of Early Christian Beliefs. Ed. David W. Bercot. (Peabody, MA: Hendrickson, 1998) 451.
47 Bercot, 450.
48 "The Epistle of Barnabas" in The Ante-Nicene Fathers: Translations of the Fathers Down to A.D. 325, 10 volumes, Alexander Roberts and James Donaldson, editors. (Grand Rapids, MI: Eerdmans Publishing, 1989.)
49 A Dictionary of Early Christian Beliefs. Ed. David W. Bercot. (Peabody, MA: Hendrickson, 1998) 451.
50 Bercot, 451.
51 Bercot, 452.
52 Currie, 6.
53 Mike Willis, "Then Cometh the End...": A Study of Eschatology. (Bowling Green, KY: Guardian of Truth Foundation, 1999) 64.
54 Franklin Littell, The Crucifixion of the Jews, p. 30. Cited in Hagee, John. Jerusalem Countdown. (Lake Mary, FL: FrontLine, 2006) 72.
55 John Hagee, Jerusalem Countdown. (Lake Mary, FL: FrontLine, 2006) 125.
56 www.jvim.com [accessed March 4, 2008].
57 Paul L. Maier quote for Hanegraaff, Hank. The Apocalypse Code. (Nashville, TN: Thomas Nelson, 2007).
58 Stephen Sizer, Christian Zionism: Road-map to Armageddon? (Downers Grove, IL: IVP Academic, 2004) 34.
59 Sizer, 53.
60 Human Rights Watch says, "Palestinians are the world's oldest and largest refugee population, and make up more than one-fourth of all refugees" (http://hrw.org/doc/?t=refugees&document [accessed December 26, 2006]).
61 William W. Baker, Theft of a Nation. (West Monroe, LA: Jireh Publications, 1989) 2, 5.
62 John Hagee, Jerusalem Countdown. (Lake Mary, FL: FrontLine, 2006) 126-127.
63 John Hagee, Jerusalem Countdown. (Lake Mary, FL: FrontLine, 2006) 45.
64 John Hagee, In Defense of Israel. (Lake Mary, FL: FrontLine, 2007) 2.
65 Hitchock, Mark. What Jesus Says About Earth's Final Days. (Sisters, OR: Multnomah Publishers, 2003) 28.
66 Stringer, Johnny. The Sign of Thy Coming: A Study of Matthew 24. (Bowling Green, KY: Guardian of Truth Foundation, 2001) Emphasis his.
67 Currie, David B. Rapture: The End-Times Error That Leaves the Bible Behind. (Manchester, NH: Sophia Institute Press, 2003) 64.
68 Currie, 25-26.
69 M.E. Patton, Reasons For Our Hope. (Fairmount, IN: Guardian of Truth Foundation).
70 Mike Willis, "Then Cometh The End..." A Study of Eschatology. (Bowling Green, KY: Guardian of Truth Foundation, 1999) 48.
71 Craig D. Atwood, Frank S. Mead and Samuel S. Hill. Handbook of Denominations in the United States 11th Edition. (Nashville, TN: Abingdon Press, 2001) 23.

More Bible workbooks that you can order from Spiritbuilding.com or your favorite Christian bookstore.

Inside Out (Carl McMurray)
Studying spiritual growth in bite sized pieces
Night and Day (Andrew Roberts)
Comparing N.T. Christianity and Islam
Church Discipline (Royce DeBerry)
A quarter's study on an important task for the church
Exercising Authority (John Baughn)
How we use and understand authority on a daily basis
Compass Points (Carl McMurray)
22 foundation lessons for home studies or new Christians
We're Different Because... (Carl McMurray)
A workbook on authority and recent church history
Communing with the Lord (Matthew Allen)
A study of the Lord's Supper and issues surrounding it
From Beneath the Altar (Carl McMurray)
A workbook commentary on the book of Revelation
Marriage Through the Ages (Royce & Cindy DeBerry)
A quarter's study of God's design for this part of our life
Parenting Through the Ages (Royce & Cindy DeBerry)
Bible principles tested and explained by successful parents
1 & 2 Timothy and Titus (Matthew Allen)
A workbook commentary on these letters from Paul
The Parables, Taking a Deeper Look (Kipp Campbell)
A relevant examination of our Lord's teaching stories
The Minor Prophets, Vol. 1 & 2 (Matthew Allen)
Old lessons that speak directly to us today
Esteemed of God, Studying the Book of Daniel (Carl McMurray)
Covering the man as well as the time between the testaments
What Should I Do? (Dennis Tucker)
A study that seeks Bible answers to life's important questions
Faith in Action: Studies in James (Mike Wilson)
Bible class workbook and commentary on James

The Lion is the Lamb (Andrew Roberts)
Study of the King of Kings, His glorious kingdom, & His promised return
When Opportunity Knocks (Matthew Allen)
Lessons on how to meet the Jehovah's Witness/Mormon who knock on your door
Reveal In Me... (Jeanne Sullivan)
A ladies study on finding and developing one's own talents
I Will NOT Be Lukewarm, Ppt/Teacher's Manual (Dana Burk)
A ladies study on defeating mediocrity
The Gospel of John (Cassondra Givans)
A study for women, by a woman, on this letter of John
Sisters at War (Cassondra Givans)
Breaking the generation gap between sisters in Christ
Will You Wipe My Tears? (Joyce Jamerson)
Resources to teach us how to help others through sorrow
Bridges or Barriers, w/Manual (Cindy DeBerry/Angie Kmitta)
Study encouraging harmony with younger/older sisters-in-Christ
Learning to Sing at Midnight (Joanne Beckley)
A study book about spiritual growth benefiting women of all ages
Transitions, with Ppt/Teacher's Manual (Ken Weliever)
A relevant life study for this changing age group
Snapshots: Defining Moments in a Girl's Life (Nicole Sardinas)
How to make godly decisions when it really matters
The Path of Peace (Cassondra Givans)
Relevant and important topics of study for teens
The Purity Pursuit (Andrew Roberts)
Helping teens achieve purity in all aspects of life
Paul's Letter to the Romans (Matthew Allen)
Putting righteousness by faith on an understandable level
AUTISM, In the Eye of the Hurricane (Juli Liske)
A family's journey from the shock of an autistic diagnosis to victory
For However Brief a Time (Warren Berkley)
A son's human interest tales of his father in a time now gone by
Family Bible Study Series (Ken Weliever)
A series of 16 quarters of Bible class curriculum ideas

www.ingramcontent.com/pod-product-compliance
Lightning Source LLC
Chambersburg PA
CBHW031253060726
47590CB00003B/888